THE DETROIT TIGERS READER

7 DAY
LOAN

Also by Tom Stanton

The Final Season
The Road to Cooperstown
Hank Aaron and the Home Run That Changed America

THE
Detroit
TIGERS
Reader

Edited by
Tom Stanton

Author of *The Final Season*

The University of Michigan Press | Ann Arbor

2008   2007   2006   2005   4   3   2   1

A CIP catalog record for this book is available from the British Library.

Library of Congress Cataloging-in-Publication Data

The Detroit Tigers reader / edited by Tom Stanton.
      p. cm.
   ISBN-13: 978-0-472-03017-0 (pbk. : alk. paper)
   ISBN-10: 0-472-03017-5 (pbk. : alk. paper)
   1. Detroit Tigers (Baseball team)—History—Sources.
I. Stanton, Tom, 1960–

GV875.D6D48   2005
796.357'64'0977434—dc22   2005011745

Contents

Preface

Tired of tales of that gluttonous, beer-guzzling, toothpick-legged slugger and his comrades in New York Pinstripes? Weary of a half-century's worth of babbling about the curses and hexes that annually derailed hopes in Boston and Chicago (well, no longer Boston)? Exasperated by how the Yankees, Red Sox, and Cubs have been anointed as the most colorful baseball teams in history by a confederacy of East Coast and Windy City media types?

Me, too. And here's why: The feverish adulation of those three franchises comes at the expense of *our* team, the Detroit Tigers—a team whose rich heritage pales next to no one's, yet struggles for a shard of spotlight. How is it that our ball club—an American League original and host to perhaps the greatest of all players, Ty Cobb—has come to languish in the shadow of those others? With the Yankees, it's explainable. No team, after all, has bought more championships. But what of Boston and Chicago? We've won four world titles since the Red Sox captured one prior to 2004, and it was our team—not a jilted billy goat of lore—that denied the Cubs victory in their last Fall Classic.

Detroit has had no lack of stars. Of course, there were the legends: Ty Cobb, the fierce competitor and reigning holder of the game's highest career batting average, and Al Kaline, our eighteen-time All-Star. But they weren't alone. Sam Crawford hit more triples than anyone, Harry Heilmann accumulated a batting average that remains among the ten best, and long before Roger Maris took the field Hank Greenberg nearly toppled Babe Ruth's season home-run record. At their peak, Charlie Gehringer had no peers among second basemen, Harold "Prince Hal" Newhouser and Denny McLain ruled the American League rubber, and Alan Trammell and Lou Whitaker dominated all other keystone combos. Toss in three impeccable catchers, Mickey Cochrane, Bill Freehan, and Ivan Rodriguez; a pair of sterling pitchers, Jim Bunning and Jack

Morris; a league-leading corner-man, George Kell; and Cecil Fielder, a hefty first baseman who for three years straight topped the RBI charts; and you've only skimmed the talent that has called Detroit home.

There has been no shortage of color, either. History has not forgotten "Schoolboy" Rowe and his sixteen straight wins in 1934 or rotund Bob "Fats" Fothergill, who challenged teammate Heinie Manush for the 1926 batting title, or Charlie Maxwell and his Sunday dingers or rookie Mark "The Bird" Fidrych, who for one season was the game's biggest drawing card, or Gates Brown and Ron LeFlore, who rose out of the prison system, or fun-loving Norm Cash, whose antics entertained almost as much as his home runs, or white-haired Sparky Anderson proclaiming yet another little-known minor leaguer as the next Pete Rose.

The story of the Tigers, like that of Detroit itself, is one of resilience and perseverance and patience. We average a first-place finish only once a decade, and we've gone spans of nearly a quarter century without. Many teams have won more world championships. The Yankees, yes, but also the Cardinals and the Pirates and the Dodgers and the Reds and the Athletics and others. Our world titles never come in clumps. They're scattered over time. It took thirty-five seasons before we won our first one, another ten for the second, twenty-three more for the third, and an additional sixteen for the fourth. And now two more decades have passed and we're still waiting for our fifth. But it *will* arrive someday and a new generation of Tigers fan will taste sweet victory.

Maybe that next triumph will resonate as deeply as our earlier ones, which were made more memorable and significant by their timing. The 1935 Tigers lifted our city emotionally from the depths of the Depression; the 1945 Tigers capped the end of a world war; the 1968 Tigers soothed the scars of a prior summer's race riots; and the 1984 Tigers gave our city a new title, rescuing it from a designation as the Murder Capital of the country. Our team has enhanced our sense of community and provided us potent reasons to celebrate as a people.

Our relationship to the home team is also a personal one. Detroit Tigers baseball has flowed through generations of our families.

In my case, it started with my grandfather Theodore Stankiewicz who, arriving in America from Poland in the early 1900s, learned to love the sport and cherished afternoons at Michigan and Trumbull watching Cobb and Crawford and Bobby Veach rule the outfield. Later, he took his sons, and they treasured their times there, cheering for Gehringer and Greenberg and Tommy Bridges. To this day, my eighty-five-year-old father, Joe Stanton, can recite the lineup of that first championship club. I can do the same for the premier teams of my youth, with Kaline and Willie Horton and Mickey Lolich. My sons, likewise, learned early to appreciate Trammell, Fielder, and Bobby Higginson.

It is not a unique story. If you love baseball and grew up rooting for our Tigers, you can certainly tell a similar tale. You can probably trace your own Tiger lineage and, if so, you can undoubtedly appreciate my joy at being invited by the University of Michigan Press to edit and shape this Detroit Tigers reader.

This project launched a wonderful adventure, affording me the chance to again experience magical moments and to rediscover a roster of interesting characters. It has been a challenge selecting which stories to include. Tens of thousands of pieces have been written about the Tigers. But it was humanly possible to read only a fraction of them.

My aim, above all others, was to create a collection that would be fun to read, one that might rekindle the passion for the local team that remains a central, though sometimes dormant, part of so many of us. I also wanted to capture a wide swath of baseball history. Primarily, I tapped the work of contemporary newspaper and magazine journalists. Some, like Grantland Rice and Damon Runyon, qualify as famous, but that was not a prerequisite.

Several individuals contributed advice and expertise to this project, among them my editor, Kelly Sippell; Tim Wiles and Freddy Berowski of the National Baseball Hall of Fame Library; David Poremba of the Detroit Public Library; and author Peter Morris, who graciously shared Hugh Jennings's work. Further, I am indebted, as always, to my agent, Philip Spitzer, a connoisseur of the game.

It would be presumptuous to proclaim this treasury as containing the best nonfiction writing about the Detroit Tigers. But I think it represents a fine sampling, and I hope it brings you joy. Also, if it serves to entertain or enlighten a few self-absorbed Yankees, Red Sox, or Cubs fans, that wouldn't be all bad either.

Tom Stanton

I found this letter in the library of the National Baseball Hall of Fame. It was written in January 1902 by W. H. Cobb, school superintendent of Franklin County, Georgia, to his son, Tyrus, then fifteen years old, who was visiting relatives in North Carolina. Within two years, the elder Cobb would be dead, shot—in an accident, reportedly—by his wife, Ty Cobb's mother. A year later, Cobb would debut with the Tigers.

1902

W. H. Cobb

DEAR BOY

Tyrus, Dear Boy —

The first snow of the year of account is down today. It is two inches I reckon. It is all of a round fine hail, not a single feathery flake. Some lodge on the limbs of the trees. Our wheat and oats have stood the winter all right. Wheat is up nicely. We are all snowed in today, principally on account of the cold weather.

Hardly a sound has been heard today. It is nearly six o'clock. I knew the past cold weather would furnish you with some fine scenery up there and I am glad you have been receptive of its austere beauty and solemn grandeur, as to color, sound, and picturesque contour or outline. That is a picturesque and romantic country with solitude enough to give nature a chance to be heard in the soul. The presence of man and the jargon of artificiality and show do not crowd out the grand aspect of God's handiwork among those everlasting hills covered

Ty Cobb

with its primeval forest, nor hush the grand oratorios of the winds, nor check the rush of her living, leaping waters.

To be educated is not only to be master of the printed page but . . . able to catch the messages of star, rock, flower, bird, painting and symphony. To have eyes that really see, ears that really hear and an imagination that can construct the perfect from a fragment. It is truly great to have a mind that will respond to and open the door of the soul to all the legions of thoughts and symbols of knowledge and emotions that the whole universe around us brings to us.

Be good and dutiful, conquer your anger and wild passions that would degrade your dignity and belittle your manhood. Cherish all the good that springs up in you. Be under the perpetual guidance of the better angel of your nature. Starve out and drive out the demon that lurks in all human blood and [is] ready and anxious and restless to arise and reign.

Be good.

Yours affectionately,
W. H. Cobb

In the autumn of 1909, Detroit found itself in its third consecutive World Series. But despite high expectations, the Pittsburgh Pirates, like the Chicago Cubs of 1907 and 1908, denied the Tigers the championship. This editorial, reflecting the city's disappointment, appeared on the front page of the Detroit Free Press.

1909

Detroit Free Press

DEFEATED, AGAIN

'Tis a sad, sad tale to relate, this story of the crowd of Tiger and Pirate fans that thronged the streets last night. Needless to say there were countless numbers of the former who employed the time-honored method of driving away remorse—that of drowning it out.

Mingled with the cheering Pittsburgh fans and the saddened Tiger fans, who tried hard to appear indifferent, there were scores of street merchants. Time was, before the last trouncing, when the team Tiger emblems seemed appropriate. Last night, harsh as it did sound, everybody was talking of the cut-rate prices of Tiger "souvenirs."

Pittsburgh rooters lost no time making themselves prominent. Hundreds of them apparently decided to remain in the home of their late foes, just to flaunt their banners in the faces of Detroiters, digging up the unhappy reminder of the awful smearing of the whitewash.

Even the poor sidewalks and pavements were forced to suffer under coats of whitewash, spread in such manner that it read very clearly, "Pittsburgh 3, Detroit 0."

Wild Bill Donovan of the 1909 Tigers

3

Those Pittsburgh banners which heretofore were worn with a modest appearance shone like street lamps on the lapels, sleeves, hats and canes of followers of the Smoky City athletes. Tiger banners there were, but many took the trouble of attaching them to a very inconspicuous portion of their wearing apparel—the shoes.

Outside of those who sought relief from their sorrow or tonic for their waning enthusiasm to such an extent that they were no longer able to navigate independently, the police had little trouble with the last demonstration from baseball bugs.

No extra force was required to patrol the streets, and few enthusiasts succeeded in rooting themselves to the Bastille.

It was a mournful, "it's all over, dust unto dust" crowd that filed out of the ballpark after the Pirates had finished twisting the Tigers' tails.

The coppers looked sour, the girls snappish and sad, the rooters crushed, and even the smiles on the faces of the real "sports" were wan and stingy.

The atmosphere of melancholy already had percolated throughout the city, through the medium of numerous scoreboards, and the mourners from the park and the mourners from downtown had no need to mingle words.

Years ago, Ernie Harwell pulled from the garbage of Tiger Stadium and saved for posterity books of carbon letters written by Frank Navin, owner of the Detroit Tigers. The letters are held in the Detroit Public Library's Burton Historical Collection. This one touched me. Navin was not known for his warmth, but some radiates from this note to catcher Charles Schmidt. Navin's brother Tom had recently died, which might explain the tone of the letter. Schmidt's baseball-playing days ended later in 1911.

1911

Frank Navin

LIFE IS SHORT

Friend Charlie:

I received your signed contract this A.M., and am very glad you signed it without any argument. It made me feel very good.

I will be in the South when the club is training, and I want to get you and [manager Hughie] Jennings started off alright. I want you to forget whatever little misunderstanding has occurred in the past, and I am sure Jennings will do the same. We are going to have a different kind of a ball club this year than we had last year.

Charlie, you must not expect to do all the work on the club behind the bat because the club has to have three catchers. There is no getting away from that. We must give them a fair amount of work to do because if you were to get hurt after doing all the catching we would be in bad shape for catchers. You can see that by the [Jimmy] Archer case. He did not get the work he should have had, otherwise he would have developed into a better catcher. We know what you can do, but we do not know what the others can do. For that reason you must get the idea out of

Frank Navin (*left*) with Billy Sullivan

your head that you should work every day and not be sore when Jennings works other catchers.

I am going to the training ground to see you and get you fixed up. You are an easy fellow to get along with and so is Jennings for that matter and we must all start off with the right foot forward this season. If we do that, in my opinion, we will give everyone a tough game, especially if we are able to develop a couple of pitchers, and we will get another chance at the World Series money in the fall.

I am very sorry you wrote the communication you did to the paper because it gives people an opportunity to holler when the club is going bad. You know the fans in Detroit are a funny lot. They want us to win all the games, and as soon as we do not they think I have told the boys not to. During the World Series games, when we played Pittsburgh, all the fans said I gave the boys orders not to win the games because I was betting on Pittsburgh.

I think you are laboring under the false impression when you state you are not appreciated. You are receiving as big a salary as any catcher in the American League, and that shows some appreciation.

Charlie, life is too short to be worrying about troubles that cannot be avoided. We are not here long enough to keep on continually arguing just for the sake of an argument. I feel sure we will get started on the right path this season, and that you will be happy and contented again before the opening of the season.

With kindest regards to Mrs. Schmidt and the children and yourself, I am

Yours Truly,
Frank J. Navin

Navin Field, which would later become Briggs Stadium and then Tiger Stadium, opened on April 20, 1912, days after the sinking of the Titanic. *The grand cement and steel structure stoked civic pride, as is evident in this Detroit story on the first regular-season game played in the new park.*

1912

E. A. Batchelor

A NEW HOME

There will be no further talk to the effect that Detroit isn't a good baseball town, and it probably will be several weeks before anyone informs us again that the franchise is shortly to be transferred to some other city. Nearly 26,000 fans, of whom 24,384 paid cash for the privilege of attending, proved yesterday afternoon not only that the City of the Straits is a good supporter of the national pastime but that it is one of the very best in the entire country.

Incidentally, the Tigers demonstrated that they are the sort of a ball club which deserves patronage. In spite of the baneful effects of much preliminary celebrating in which the Jungaleers nearly were killed with kindness, they wrenched a 6 to 5 victory from Cleveland after eleven innings of battling that had the fans chewing their finger nails and whooping themselves hoarse throughout the afternoon.

Only five cities in the country, New York, Chicago, Boston, Pittsburgh

Navin Field

and Philadelphia, have turned out larger crowds than that which honored the dedication of the splendid concrete stadium known as Navin Field. There were more people inside the gates than the entire population of Battle Creek as shown by the census of 1911 and only eight cities in the state have as many inhabitants as there were fans within the concrete walls of the Tigers' new home.

Every seat was taken and thousands stood around the borders of the outfield, necessitating group rules which limited the length of any hit to two bases. The assemblage was just as enthusiastic as it was big, too, and there were abundant opportunities for shouting, as the game was one of those desperately fought affairs in which each side has numerous chances to win and peril often is averted only by splendid fielding or nervy pitching or both.

George Mullin, without whose presence in the box no opening celebration in Detroit would be complete, covered himself with glory in a desperate duel with Van Gregg, star southpaw of the Davis stable. Time after time, the big fellow pitched himself out of holes from which escape had seemed impossible. To crown it all, he sent [Owen "Donie"] Bush home with the winning run, a single to short doing the work after two Tigers had perished in the eleventh. Little Ownie's hit, followed by one from the bat of the sturdy [Oscar] Stanage, paved the way for Mullin's victory-bringing trump. Cleveland's total of twelve men left on bases is in itself a striking testimonial to George's fearlessness in the many cases.

In two of the overtime innings, Detroit's chances to win weren't rated very high but Mullin's nerve was equal to the emergencies and he escaped unscathed when wholesale disaster seemed imminent.

In the tenth, one of the foes reached second base with [Ted] Easterly, a dangerous hitter, at bat. Maumee George was far too crafty to take a chance on the Cleveland backstop and purposely passed him, this strategy bringing up Gregg, who is as poor as a sticker as he is great as a pitcher. An inning later, Detroit was in even more desperate straits, Cleveland getting men on third and second with only one out and the ferocious [Larry] Lajoie at bat. Fortunately it was possible to dispose of Larry by forcing him to accept a pass, a gift that he received with very bad grace. Then Mullin went to work and got the side out on a force play at home and an easy roller to himself. Rather than risk getting into any more such pinches big George decided to wind it up in the Tigers' half of this inning.

Gregg was a foeman worthy of the Tiger veteran's steel. Like his conqueror, he often was in trouble and only his ability to pitch great ball in pinches enabled him to prolong the contest to its overtime limit. The young left-hander was unfortunate in that the Jungaleers bunched their hits on him in four innings, getting three in the first, two in the third, three in the eighth and three in the eleventh. As there was scoring in all of these periods it will be seen that the Tigers got rich return for their labors.

Each side made an even dozen hits. Mullin passed four men, two of them purposely, while Gregg let three escape without intending to do so. In fielding the Naps had it on us considerably, making but two errors while Detroit is charged with five. There were, however, a number of bad plays on the Naps' infield which do not show in the tabulated list of stumblings. [Terry] Turner several times was too ambitious and, by deflecting bounders, spoiled plays that [Ivy] Olson probably would have made if let alone. The veteran "Topsey's" mistakes in judgment usually came in pinches, too.

Naturally much of the interest of the fans centered around the work of [Ossie] Vitt and [Baldy] Louden, the only strangers in the Tiger lineup. In the case of Vitt everybody went home fully convinced that the club has picked up a very rare jewel among athletes. The "little" fellow from San Francisco got three clean hits, scored two runs and did himself proud in the field. His success won him thousands of friends and toward the latter part of the game he was given an ovation every time he went out to his position.

Louden didn't do so well, though his two sacrifice hits had a very useful place in the day's attainments. He failed to get a hit, but took good care of six fielding chances, including a couple of difficult ones.

Baseball's brightest luminary, Tyrus R. Cobb, of course, could not let an opportunity of displaying his charms to 26,000 persons pass so he put on the whole show with a few interpolated numbers for good measure. A whole column could be written on the Peach's performance alone and even a bare list of his feats takes up considerable space. He got two hits, stole two bases, including home, failed by a very small margin in an attempt to perform his favorite stunt of scoring from second on an infield out and made two catches in center field that were easily the defensive features of the game.

In the first inning, Ty and Sam Crawford twice worked the double steal, the first time with third and second as their goals and the next with the plate as the point assailed by the flying Georgian. The steal of home was as clean as a whistle, Easterly being unable to grab Gregg's high pitch and apply it to the Cobb person until he had slid safely across the rubber.

In weight of slugging that king of main-strength club artists, Sam Crawford, was the day's best bet. Two singles and a double, which would have been a triple at least and probably a homer but for the restricting ground rules, were Sam's contributions to the crowd's happiness. As already mentioned, he followed hard on the heels of Cobb in two double thefts in the same inning.

Larry Lajoie showed himself to be an athlete for whom vast and hostile throngs have no terrors. He played a beautiful fielding game and was on the bases five of the six times that he faced Mullin, twice on errors, once when Mullin walked him purposely and twice on clean hits, the second of which was a double into the left field crowd. Joe Jackson, Cleveland's other first magnitude star, didn't do anything startling, making only one hit. Twice he was thrown out on the infield and once lifted an easy fly while the other two times up he got four balls.

Detroit's errors were particularly costly, three of the Naps' runs being directly due to them, while four men reached first base either on fumbles or bad throws. The grounds are in rather bad shape as might be expected, so it is unjust to criticize fielders too harshly. The Tigers have had no more chances than their adversaries to learn the lay of the land and that they are assessed more misplays is due to bad luck more than anything else.

It seemed Cleveland had no trouble whatever in getting men as far as third base but found the path from that cushion to the place where they pay off beset with difficulties. Half a dozen men wearing the Davis gray reached the next-to-last stage without living to gain the ultimate corner, which shows that Mullin wasn't given to fits of nervousness nor trembling at the knees.

The Tigers, on the other hand, made a very few threats that didn't result in some action that gave work to the scoreboard operator, though Gregg several times ended their run-making sooner than the maniacs in the big stands liked.

After the Board of Commerce committee had presented a fine flag to the club and Mayor Thompson had pitched the first ball with Charlie Bennett behind the bat and Sam Thompson as umpire, the vast throng settled itself to enjoy the day's real action. . . .

When this profile appeared in Baseball Magazine, *Ty Cobb was the game's most celebrated player. At age thirty, he had already won nine consecutive batting titles. Typical of sports reporting in the day, this story provided a glossy portrait of Cobb.*

1916

F. C. Lane

A DAY WITH COBB

All night I had been riding through the heart of Dixie on a rheumatic old sleeper that groaned and bounded at every joint in the rusty rails. Indistinctly through the intervals of a broken sleep I recalled Sherman's famous march through Georgia and his celebrated remarks thereon. And the truth of those remarks was fairly jostled into my bones. Somewhat wayworn and threadbare in spirit, "early on a frosty mornin'" I dismounted at Augusta.

With one hand hastily inserted in my overcoat and the other on my grip I wended my way into the station and asked for a city directory. The attendant looked at me vaguely and remarked, in a far-off voice, that they had none. A friend, who was lounging near chewing tobacco with great industry, offered the suggestion that they might have one in the baggage room.

In this receptacle of battered trunks I found two or three human beings, one of

Ty Cobb and his children

whom produced from beneath a crushing load of papers and nondescript refuse a moth-eaten directory.

"Ca," "Ci," my eye wandered down the "C's" till I stopped opposite a familiar name in the "Co.'s."

"William Street?" I queried. "What car do I take to go to William Street?"

The minion of Southern transportation gazed vacantly at me. "What part of William Street do you want to go to?" he asked.

"I don't know," I replied. "The page is torn here, but I want to see Ty Cobb." Instantly there was a transformation in that inanimate posture.

"Ty Cobb!" The baggage-man straightened up and repeated the syllables after me with a world of respect. "Ty Cobb!" the listening assistants echoed. "We think a good deal of Ty Cobb down here," repeated the baggage-man, and then he proceeded to tell me with the most painstaking exactness just how I should reach that home, which is the most treasured spot in Augusta.

In due time, no doubt from an Augusta standpoint, a trolley car appeared in sight. I entered and told the dreamy-eyed conductor that I wished to alight at William Street.

"William Street," he murmured vacantly. "That can't be on my route. I never heard of it."

"They told me in the baggage-room that this was the right line to take to reach Ty Cobb," I remonstrated.

"Ty Cobb!" said the conductor. "Oh, I know where he lives all right. Couldn't tell you the name of the street but I know the house. We go quite near it. You can see it from the car window. I will point it out to you when we get there."

It isn't the glare of publicity which shows a well-known personage in his proper light. It is rather the tiny rays that are thrown upon his character, the little things which indicate him as he is. And these two trivial experiences will show as clearly as anything else how Ty Cobb is esteemed among his neighbors.

"A prophet is not without honor save in his own town" is often true of a ballplayer. Greenville doesn't exactly enthuse at the name of Joe Jackson. Carnegie, Penn., doesn't knock off work when Hans Wagner comes to town. The wheels keep right on moving at Meriden, Conn., when Ed Walsh and Jack Barry are away. But Augusta, Ga., has incorporated Ty Cobb in the city charter. His fame is her fame. His friends are her friends. And if perchance Ty Cobb has enemies, and so strong-minded an individual as he could scarcely help having enemies, they had best remain away from the genial Southern city on the Savannah River.

After climbing sundry hills and descending valleys equally numerous I was beginning to wonder if Ty Cobb had moved out of the state when the conductor whistled. Not being used to that kind of a signal I looked around and saw that he was motioning me to alight. "That's his house over there among the trees," he said and pulled the bell rope.

The Cobb home is a typical Southern mansion with a great broad veranda running about it, an easy display of room which lends an hospitable air to the mansion most in keeping with the character of its inmates. I didn't have time to ring the bell for Ty himself had the door open and was extending his hand in welcome while I was still mounting the steps. His huge car was throbbing and pulsating in the road beside the house all ready, I imagined, to take its owner on one of his many excursions into the hills. But Ty himself explained the situation by saying that he had just called off a hunting trip that minute. I trust that such was the case and that the courteous host was not inconvenienced in his plans by my unexpected visit.

Hero worship is quite as much a part of normal life as eating three meals a day. We all respect men who have accomplished things above the ordinary. There are men who have done great deeds who never allow that fact to be crowded into the background. Face to face they are distant still. But anyone who meets the greatest ballplayer who ever wore a uniform will see only a vivacious young American full of life and enthusiasm and good cheer, and they will never glean from his unaided conversation that he ever accomplished anything whatever.

There are swell-headed ballplayers, we regret to say, just as there are individuals suffering from that distressing malady in all walks of life. But Ty Cobb is not one of them. On the field he isn't overly popular, perhaps. There is an undercurrent of envy in human nature which is sufficient to account for that. When Cobb is at bat or on the bases there is an all but uncontrollable impulse to show him up if possible. And Cobb is not an easy man to converse with in the heat of action. But although aggressive and audacious to the verge of desperation, he is not swell-headed. And off the field he is as democratic and easy to meet as anyone could wish.

But let us check up a day from the diary of the game's most famous player.

Ty gets up when he happens to feel like it. If he is going hunting the hour is the uncanny one of 3 A.M. or maybe earlier. If he hasn't anything particular in mind he gets up at 8 o'clock or later. Eating cuts no great figure in the Cobb establishment. Ty is so thoroughly a ballplayer, with the peculiarities of the craft, that he carries the summer habit of two meals a day right through the winter as well. If the fiery Ty needs only two meals when he is beating out lean bunts by lightning speed or playing a dazzling game in the field why should he need more in the season of rest?

An automobile is as Ty's right hand, and he has a good one, a high-power car that chugs with disgust at the hills of the neighborhood. When Ty wants to go anywhere he is always in a hurry and the car can't go any too fast to take him there. But the engine is already panting for action.

We are off. Our first stop is at the country club. This fine building is set amid rolling hills, commanding a grand sweep of country and has, so it is said, one of the best golf links in the South. "In the winter I am inclined to slight my game a little," says Ty, "for I am no enthusiast at golf. I like the game and see its advantages. It is good exercise, develops control over the muscles and benefits a player who has to bat for a living a good deal as batting practice does. The swing is different, the utensils used are different and you slug at a stationary ball instead of a moving one. And yet you have to hit right in either case and I believe playing golf helps a man's game at baseball."

Sometimes Ty tarries a while and follows the course around the golf links. Sometimes he stays only a few minutes to talk for a moment with some acquaintance—everyone knows him—and then speeds away to town. There, although Augusta is a thriving city of nearly 60,000 inhabitants, everyone knows him as well. People hail him from the sidewalks, crossing the streets, from other vehicles, everywhere. Ty's progress through town is a continuous revue.

But there are certain vantage points where he is most likely to be found. One of these is the office of a local dentist. Here several choice spirits hang out and Ty is a frequent visitor.

A particular hobby of the Georgian is dogs. While I was there he had a dog which was away at boarding school being trained for etiquette, table manners or something of the kind. Cobb was interested in current events, still more so in baseball happenings, but most of all in that particular dog. One of the men in the office was training the dog, a sort of private tutor, and they had a long animated discussion as to what should be done with this particular canine so as to make a good bird dog out of him at the earliest possible moment. My own knowledge of dogs, which extends just far enough to distinguish a bulldog from a greyhound, was not particularly illumined by the conversation. But that it was an unusually able and weighty one was well attested by the vigor with which Ty argued his point.

From the atmosphere of dogs and quail we proceeded to a music store. Next to four-footed beasts Cobb loves music. Well remembering a time last summer when he appeared late at a game in New York because he had to stop to hear the grand organ at Aeolian Hall, I was not surprised.

In this establishment Cobb had a friend as usual, a friend who was a composer. He played two of his own compositions, which Cobb criticized as frankly as he criticizes an umpire's decisions.

"I have often wished I could become a composer," said Ty in a retrospective mood as we whirled rapidly away, "but I don't suppose I have any talent along that line. Every man to his trade, and I guess mine is cut out for me. Baseball is a new game and you don't read in history of any men who became immortal by becoming great players. But any bid to anything out of the ordinary in my own case will be won on the diamond or not at all. And I know enough of fame on the diamond to realize that it lasts just as long as the ability is there to win it. I shall have my day like all the rest, and whatever I have done will be forgotten just as other records have been forgotten before. I always was ambitious, I guess. I used to think that if I were ever able to make a record on the diamond I would be satisfied. But people have been good enough to claim I have done no less and I am not satisfied."

"What will you do when you are through with baseball?" I ventured.

"I have often asked myself that question and I have never gotten any answer which was quite satisfactory," said Ty, "but I suppose I will follow the line of least resistance and settle down to a quiet, uneventful life in the country, living all the year round much the same as I am living today."

"You might go into politics," I suggested.

"No," he smiled and shook his head. "Assuming I had any talent for the job I don't think I would like it. But I have no reason to suppose I have any talent along that line. And I can't write and I can't compose music, and what is there that I could do? Nothing that I know of, save a humdrum life in the country. It looks rather welcome now for I get so much of the other kind, but I suppose I will get tired of it after I have lived it a while.

"I would like to travel, I think, when this war is over. They are making history now and we are living in the very pages that will afterward be written. Some day it will be worthwhile to walk over these great battlefields where the war is being fought out and I want to do that very thing. No, I haven't any decided notions in favor of either side. I believe the conflict was inevitable, according to the system followed by both parties in Europe. Someday, sooner or later, there was bound to be a crash and it came rather sooner than most people expected.

"I went on the stage once. I didn't know but that it would be an interesting life. Of course, I didn't deceive myself into supposing I had any special ability as an actor but I thought the life might be worthwhile. Maybe if a man could live without sleep and was made of cast iron it might be. But I found it hard, so hard that I want no more of it. I have passed up good offers since then, good from the financial standpoint. But I reasoned 'what is the use?' I am no hog. I am making money enough, money that with commonsense will be all that I shall need. When I am through with the game, unless I experience some hard luck, which I can't foresee now, I shall be independent and able to give my family a home and my children an education. The active season is enough for the whole year, for I don't get my money for nothing. There is a great deal expected and if I have one or two bad days I know how the grumbling grows. A man has to deliver all the time and the more he is paid the more he has to deliver. I am pretty tired and stale when the season is over and if I risked my health through the winter for a few thousand dollars where would I get off in the long run? No, I settled all that for myself a long while ago. If I were a young ballplayer just breaking in and had a chance to earn money on the side I would take every dollar I could get. But in my present circumstances I turn them all down. There is nothing in it. The man who tries to do too much doesn't do anything right."

Occasionally as we dashed through the streets Cobb would indicate a building. "I have an interest in that," he would say.

"Most of your money is in real estate?" I asked.

"Yes," he answered. "I like real estate and bank stock. I just invested a little money in some bank stocks a while ago. I think it is a good investment."

There is one room in the Cobb house which is always under lock and key. Ty carries the key. It is his room and its contents are never disturbed. A picture of that room would be worthwhile when he unlocked the door and escorted me across its forbidden portals.

A mass of accumulated pictures, guns, trophies of the chase, a thousand and one knick-knacks lay scattered in profusion on the bureaus and the bookcases and the floor. On the shelf was a silver-hinged cigar box full of dollar cigars, which a friend gave him for a present. "They're fine cigars," commented Ty, "though ten-centers are more in my line. What I brought you in for was to show you these books. I am a bug on Napoleon. Yes, that bottle up there is full of whiskey, moonshine whiskey, that a friend gave me. Patronize home products, you know. About Napoleon, I have all the books on his life that I ever heard of. I made a resolve to read two hours a day through the winter, but I don't always do it. So many things come up. But when I do read I find that I am most interested in Napoleon. He was a remarkable man. I never tire of digging up something about his life.

"That drawer is full of letters. Lots of people write to me. I don't know why. It bothers me more than any other one thing in the winter, those letters. I can't answer all of them. It would take too much time. I have thought of having a secretary. I guess I will have to get one if I ever catch up with my correspondence but I have about given up hope. It bothers me, too, because I have the feeling that I am always neglecting someone."

Ty's parlor, drawing room, or whatever he calls it, is a spacious apartment. It might well serve for an entire city flat. A fireplace warmed the room and seemed to revive the reminiscent mood in which he fell when we seated ourselves before its welcome glow.

"I get into a lot of trouble by speaking too plainly," commented Ty. "I have made enemies by it, I suppose, but my philosophy is brief. I claim that life is too short to be diplomatic. A man's friends won't mind what he says when they know his way, and those who are not his friends don't count. That's the way I look at it. I am glad this baseball war is all over.* I guess everybody is, but I can see it will make trouble for the ballplayers. A good many people think the players have been having things too easy. Perhaps some of them have, but I have never seen a great deal of it in my experience. I know how hard I had to work to get a raise from $2,200 to $2,700 a year, and that was when I was leading the league in batting, too. Of course I got the big money later on, but I had been in the game some years and playing at top speed before I got it.

[In 1915, a third major league, the short-lived Federal League, had challenged the National and American circuits. —Ed.]

"The men in the Federal League were fine fellows so far as I saw them. Mr. Sinclair and Mr. Gilmore wanted me to join them and treated me royally. They made me some great offers, offers that I couldn't pass by without careful thought. But they had everything against them and from my own selfish reasons there was every consideration in the world which urged me to stay where I was. Other things being equal, as Walter Johnson says, a player gives his home club preference and the same thing goes for his league. I had made my record in the American League and preferred to stay there even though I could command a larger salary elsewhere.

"President Navin got worried, however. We have had our share of tilts, Navin and I, but I will say for him that he has used me well and I intend to do the same by him so far as I can. Still I always had sense enough to realize that it was purely a matter of business, that he would get his players to work for as little as possible and the players would try to get as much as possible. It is the old story of labor and capital, of supply and demand.

"He came to me one day and said, 'I would like to have you strike the ten-days clause out of my contract.' At that time the Federal League was making a great fight on that particular point and most of the organized club owners shook out the clause from their contracts, usually paying well for the privilege.

"I said to him, 'Why do you want the clause stricken out?'

"'I am beginning to think that maybe the contract isn't binding just as it is written with that clause in,' he answered.

"'Well,' I said, 'this is rather a late day to find it out. And if what you say is true, it means that I haven't had any claim on you since I have been working for you.'

"'That may be,' said Navin, 'but let's get together and fix it up now.'

"'Well,' I said, 'I don't see any rush about it. If you have been holding me over a trap door for nine years I ought to have the same privilege for a few days at least.'

"He didn't say any more at the time, but he came to me a few days later with much the same story. I suppose it was extremely cruel to keep him in suspense, but I couldn't resist the temptation.

"But after he had mentioned the topic several times I said to him, 'It seems to me that you are pretty much concerned about this thing. I haven't asked you to take that clause out of my contract or to alter it in any way. I am still operating under the contract and have no complaint to make. I am satisfied but you don't seem to be. Now if that is the case and you want the contract altered it must be for some reason, and it must be worth something to you. Of course if you look at it in that light, it is my business to work for money, and I am open to reason—just what is your proposition?'

"I will tell you what his proposition was and I will let you see the contract. But I will ask you not to give out its contents."

And here Ty ran upstairs, two at a time as is his usual custom, and speedily returned with the document.

I will, of course, respect his wishes. The contents of his contract are as safe with me as they were on the original document. But for the curiosity of the public I will say that that contract called for a greater salary than was ever paid a ballplayer before, greater by a considerable margin than the highest salary, real or fictitious, ever ascribed to any other player.

As I scanned that contract I recalled the conversation I had had with Ban Johnson in the season when Ty Cobb was holding out for $15,000. Ban had showed more heat about the matter than is his wont, and just before I left he said, "If Cobb is waiting for the American League to pay him $15,000, he might just as well stay down in Georgia and pick cotton. The American League can afford to pay no such salaries."

But times change. In the American League Walter Johnson is reputed to draw a salary somewhat above $15,000 a year. So is Tris Speaker, while Collins' salary is supposed to equal that stupendous figure. But whether or not these famous stars draw the money they are reputed to draw Ty Cobb surmounts them all by a wide margin.

Recalling this episode Ty laughed. "I did stay out for a while before we came to terms," he said, "and I didn't find that the experience cost me money. I played in the neighborhood of twenty exhibition games and my share of the receipts was well over $2,000. The last game I played, if I remember, I took in over $400. So I lost nothing while the Detroit club was formulating the contract they were willing to give me. Of course I couldn't expect to keep up at this figure indefinitely, but I did pretty well as long as I worked at it."

Mrs. Ty Cobb, whom her husband calls "Charlie," is a woman of uncommon judgment and good sense. With a husband as high strung and temperamental as hers it is well that she is. A man of Cobb's quick, nervous disposition hasn't the most placid temperament in the world.

Cobb's two children partake of the family characteristics. The daughter, Shirley, is Ty's special favorite, a quiet little maid of four years, with much of her mother's even disposition. Shirley always accompanies her father and he lets her steer the wheel of his big car for half-minute intervals on a smooth road. The son, Ty Junior, is more high strung, more "like his old man," as Ty says.

Ty is particularly anxious lest his son grow up and become a mollycoddle. With his tutelage there is scant danger, as an incident in the young man's education (he is six years old) will show.

The youthful Ty got into an argument one day with another boy, and his visitor gave him every cause to feel resentment. Ty overheard the argument, and convinced that his son was not standing up for his rights, he called him aside. "Now," he said, "that boy may be older than you but he is no bigger. He has insulted you and if you don't go out and lick him I will lick you." Ty Junior, duly impressed by such logic, lived up to the reputation of his father in strenuous manner, and since that time there has never been any doubt of his wish or ability to insist on his rights.

Ty himself is of an aggressive, scrappy and hot-headed temperament. He has been in numerous scrimmages and no doubt will be in many more. But it is all a part of the day's work to him, a necessary adjunct of the strenuous life he leads and the various people—good, bad and indifferent—with whom he is unavoidably thrown in contact.

By way of illustrations two of Ty's historic scraps might be mentioned—one in which he assaulted a spectator in New York who had used abusive language, a scrap which resulted in the celebrated strike of the Detroit players and was indirectly instrumental in bringing about the Players' Fraternity.

Another was with a butcher in Detroit whom Ty thought had insulted Mrs. Cobb. This notable tilt for honor resulted in a sprained thumb and a sprained batting record for Ty.

But Cobb's scrappiness is really but an overflow of his nervous spirits. The man who is the greatest player the game has ever known must, perforce, be hung on steel wires, must fairly scintillate with nervous energy.

Ty is always in the forefront of progress and anxious to try out a new thing. A year ago he made a flight in an aeroplane, a flight that was little heralded at the time, to be sure, but one which he speaks about now with evident relish. "It was quite an experience," he said. "It happened at Pensacola and a little Frenchman, the crack man of the place, took me up. I can't say that I would like the sport as a steady diet, but one voyage was interesting. I noticed that every once in a while the machine would seem to skid a bit, if I may use that word, though there wasn't anything to skid upon but air. It would jump and duck apparently a foot or two, and I

commented on that fact when we alighted. 'A foot or two,' said the aston-
ished aeronaut. 'When we struck those air pockets, we would drop sometimes fifteen or twenty feet. That's what seemed like a foot or two.'"

"Which one of your records do you prize most of all?" I asked Cobb
in an effort to turn his mind to baseball themes.

"Which one would you expect?" he asked.

"The time when you batted for .420?" He shook his head.

"That was a great record," I argued. "They said no one would ever bat
.400 again."

"It's medium hard to hit .400," Ty conceded with a smile, "but I don't
think most of that."

"The time you stole ninety-six bases?" I suggested.

"It's not easy to steal ninety-six bases," admitted Ty. "You can't let the
grass grow under your feet. A man has to get on base a good many times
to steal ninety-six. You can figure it out yourself. He has to bat well or get
a lot of bases on balls or both to reach first often enough to steal ninety-
six bases and then he has to have a number of other things break in his
favor. If I had known at the beginning of the season that I was going to
steal ninety-six bases I should have tried to take an extra spurt and made
it an even hundred. I think I could have added four somewhere along
the line, but, of course, I couldn't foresee the final score."

"The time you made 248 hits in a single season?" I asked.

"No," he said.

"The time when you scored 147 runs?"

"No. I won't keep you guessing any longer," he said. "The record that
means most to me, and I will confess as much, is the record of leading
the league nine years in succession. It has never been done before, and
that is the hardest one of all from my way of thinking. A player getting
everything in his favor and gaining a good start can burn things up for a
season. But to hit at top speed for nine years running is a different thing
again. I think if I am well that I have my eye on that little old ball for one
year more, to make it an even ten. I think I can count on that, though
there is no telling the opposition I may strike. After that I don't care so
much. We all have our stint unconsciously perhaps. We all aim at a certain mark and when we hit it, if we do, we ought to be satisfied. That is
my mark, my ambition to lead the league for ten successive seasons. And
the thing I have done which means the most to me is that I have come
within one of it already."

There was not the slightest trace of boastfulness in Ty's manner.
There never is. He talked in a quiet, earnest way just as an amateur would

talk of improving his game of golf. He was speaking of a record that has never been made, that if he succeeds in reaching, he will hold alone against the field. But that was part of his day's work, breaking records. That is what he is supposed to do. Yes, other players are paid to make hits and runs and putouts, but Ty Cobb is the one player who is paid to make and break records—and he does it.

A tour of the yard to see the dogs (the smallest one was extremely affectionate. "The runt," said Ty. "He needs more attention than the others."); a visit to the barn to go through some of his things in search for pictures; a casual word to Uncle Joe, who does the chores; and I was obliged to remind Ty that the train would soon be leaving.

"This is the way I live," said he, while we sped to the station. "A good many people come to see me. Those silver cups in the house were given to me by friends. That autograph picture of President Wilson was given me by the President before he was elected while on a trip to Augusta. But this is a typical day. Always glad to see my friends—you know, to hunt or lounge around or play golf as the occasion requires. The winter is soon over and then another season's grind begins. Some of the players kick because I don't get much spring training. But I get my training right here. I am a little heavy now—weigh 192—but I don't take on weight very much. Pretty soon I will play golf every day more and more, and when I join the club I will be in prime shape. As it is, I get stale before the season is over. What would I get if I added a long training trip grind to my regular work? It isn't because I am lazy that I don't like training trips. It is because I know I wouldn't do my best work if I had to take them. President Navin understands, and he approves of my course, so why should anyone else care?

"Those northern cities are hard places to spend winter in," sympathized Ty as I dismounted to the platform. "I stayed one year at Detroit. It was enough. If I had to live there I would get pneumonia. The sunny south is good enough for me, not that the Yankees aren't all right in the summer time. Couldn't get along without them, you know, and the war is a long time over down here." And he laughed. "No, you needn't hurry for the train. This isn't New York. Nobody hurries in Augusta. So long, I'll see you next summer," and he waved a goodbye from the platform as the train slowly pulled out from the station, bringing to a close a most enjoyable day with baseball's greatest player.

Reprinted from Baseball Magazine, *April 1916.*

The son of a millionaire squanders his opportunities but then, recognizing his erroneous ways, straightens his life out and redeems himself. In the first half of the twentieth century, baseball writers often unearthed such tales as lessons in living for the baseball-loving boys of America. This non-bylined piece from Baseball Magazine *appeared in the winter of 1917 after "Tub" Spencer had returned to the major leagues following a four-season break. Spencer hit .370 in fifty-four at-bats, leading to this glowing pronouncement. His success, however, soon evaporated. He batted .240 in 1917 and .219 in 1918, ending his career.*

1917

Baseball Magazine

A BASEBALL ROMANCE

The real baseball romance of 1916, with, no doubt, a brilliant chapter added for next season? The real baseball "thriller" of the year, with a lesson in every line, an example to American youth, and a message of hope to the weak and wavering? The comeback of Edward Spencer, catcher, now the pet backstop of Detroit, and the backbone of the Tiger team for 1917!

There have been few baseball romances like that of "Tub" Spencer—and the best chapters of Spencer's melodrama are yet to come. Way back in 1907, the scouts of the St. Louis Browns unearthed no less than three star catchers, all at one time, in the Texas League: Jim Stephens, Branch Rickey, and Ed Spencer. Rickey was destined to play both in St. Louis and New York, to become a manager of a big league team, and to make a pleasing record as a corking good athlete and a high-class college gentleman. Stephens caught in the big show for quite a while, but finally went back, and drifted into baseball obscurity. Both

The Tigers thought Tub Spencer might succeed Oscar Stanage (*above*).

Rickey and Stephens had interesting histories, but neither of them had a life-romance to match that of Eddie Spencer.

When Spencer came up to the big league, he was a college graduate, already famed for his joyous and convivial ways at school. Ere long Spencer's merry-making became the talk of the American League, but his baseball value was so great that he was seldom disciplined. He was a second Ewing, so they all declared—a mighty catcher whose rifle-throws to second turned them back halfway down the trail; whose intelligence and skill behind the bat were almost uncanny; and who hit that ball with tremendous power. "Tub" Spencer—they soon began to call him that, for the boy fast put on bulgy and unwieldy flesh—was a rich young man, son of a millionaire; he had always done what he wished at college and in the minor league; baseball, to Eddie Spencer, was not a livelihood, but a joy ride and a pastime—and why should he take baseball seriously?

And so Spencer kept on in the big league, the rolls of fat encroaching fast upon his figure, his keen eye growing dimmer, his matchless arm beginning to grow slow. It was all great sport for Spencer—but it couldn't last forever. One day came his notice of release—and then the boy woke up. Woke up, it seemed, too late, for his folks at home, exasperated by the stories that they heard, had turned him down—had told him to go along upon the trail he had selected. Almost in a day, the Millionaire Kid was jobless and money-less—the champagne dream was over.

For awhile, there were occasional paragraphs concerning Spencer and his wanderings. Fat and wheezy, penniless and useless, he went here and there, picking up his living as he could. Then—Spencer disappeared. Vanished from view; removed himself from the world that had used him so hospitably and so hard. Vanished for a year and more.

Tub Spencer, the fallen idol of the college crowds and the big league fans, had gone up into the mountains of the far Northwest. Alone in the solitudes he wrestled with his troubles—and he won. He scrambled up and down the crags, he hunted in the valleys. Day by day his eye grew clearer and pouched fat came off his mighty frame. Never did a man have a harder fight to make, but Edward Spencer, out there in the hills, made his fight and won it.

One day a powerful athlete, still young, clear-eyed and active, turned up behind the bat in a club of the Pacific League. It was Tub Spencer, a tub no longer, but even stronger, even faster, than the great young catcher who had come up from the Texas League so many years before.

His work in the Pacific League was super fine, and the big league managers soon began to eye him wonderingly, almost bewildered at the possibility of such a comeback. Over at Detroit, the catching staff was weakening—its mainstay, Oscar Stanage, was growing old, its younger maskers were inadequate to the work thrust upon them. And so Detroit sent for Edward Spencer, and Spencer, late in the 1916 season, came again into his own.

Over at Detroit they count on great things from Ed Spencer next summer. Owner [Frank] Navin says that he will be the mainstay of the team, and that he shall have a salary to match. Spencer says he isn't worrying about the salary. He has been taken back into the home circle just as he has been taken back into the big league; he is a rich man again, and the baseball pay is little to him now. But there's this great difference: Nine years ago, Ed Spencer didn't need the salary because he had money and baseball was a joyride, anyhow. Today, Ed Spencer doesn't need the salary but he wants to show the baseball world what a man he has become and he'll stick to the great game till the cows come home.

Few baseball heroes, once the thick fat has gathered on their bones and their speed has gone, have ever made the good fight and won clear through. Spencer made the fight and made it win. He deserves full credit, not alone for all he did to help himself back into the big league camp but for the example he has set for others.

Reprinted from Baseball Magazine, *April 1917.*

In April 1917, the U.S. Congress and President Woodrow Wilson committed America to the battle being waged in Europe. A month later, before U.S. troops landed overseas and became embroiled in what would later be known as World War I, the Chicago Tribune *tried to inspire citizens with this editorial referencing the Detroit ball club.*

1917

Chicago Tribune

TO WAR

Half of Ty Cobb's value lies in the fact that when he steps to the plate with the stick, he knows for a certainty that he surely can paste that pill. Cobb is half conviction and half accomplishment. He would have a tenth of the accomplishment if he did not have the conviction.

It is an unromantic fashion in which to approach the ordeal of war by referring to a man who day after day goes about a professional duty with an intense desire to do that duty well, for himself and for his ball team.

But the spirit which sends Cobb to bat determined to make the hit which brings in the winning run or starts the winning rally is, modified to the expressions necessary for the sporting pages, the spirit which Henry V voiced when he asked the English archers and pike men to go once more into the breach, dear friends, and remember that upon St. Crispin's eve thereafter the silken gentlemen who remained at home

would feel the curse of their softness and that the iron men who could show scars would show them proudly at the fireside.

Henry of England would have loved to have Cobb or Jennings at his side when he prepared the small English army for its work at Agincourt. He had in remembrance Crecy and Poictiers. He had to do as well as his progenitors.

We have now to do as well as our progenitors did at Cold Harbor. Henry V had to do as well as the English in the other century had done and Shakespeare represents him as a Hughie Jennings on the sidelines.

The fellows had to win. Poetry may decorate their emotions, but history yields to their achievement. It was the will to win, stimulated by shrewd evangelistic work, such as the United States must have now.

We need to understand that the American eagle must find the sky free for his flights or the American people will cower in their cellars. Either strong Americans will win with bayonets or weak Americans will be pulling out their pocketbooks. Either we kill the enemy or pay him.

There is no other course open to the American republic in their war. The enemy is defeated or indemnified. We either attack as Ty Cobb attacks or we pay as a solvent but reluctant debtor meets his creditors.

There can be no happiness in paying tribute. The joy of the battle may be overemphasized, but it certainly is a pleasanter emotion than that which attends the reluctant drawing out of the purse strings at a conqueror's command.

We may love ease and slippers, but we do not love humiliation. There is no American who would like to draw upon his bank account to make up a sum demanded by a foreign commander who had told his city that a certain large sum of money must be provided within twenty-four hours.

If we do not like such prospects we must work to avoid them. They are imminent in the world just now. We need the spirit of Ty Cobb and Hughie Jennings and Joan of Arc. We do not care how good the pitching is—and the Germans are wonderful pitchers—we intend to make the seventh inning rally and get in the winning runs. Let the other fellow go dejected to the clubhouse. We shall not need our end of the ninth inning. The game will be over when our time comes for that.

Copyright 1917, Chicago Tribune.

Hall of Famer Hughie Jennings managed the Tigers longer than anyone other than Sparky Anderson. His cast of characters included Ty Cobb, Sam Crawford, and the beloved "Germany" Schaefer, whom Jennings wrote about in his column "Rounding Third."

1925

Hugh Jennings

GERMANY THE JOKESTER

Among the men usually named as great second basemen you will not find the name of Herman (Germany) Schaefer. He was not a good fielder and he was not a good hitter. As a matter of fact, I would not say that he came up to the major league average at either. And yet Schaefer was one of the most valuable ball players I have ever seen. It was Schaefer, more than Cobb, Crawford, Donovan or any other star of that outfit, that gave Detroit pennants in the seasons of 1907 and 1908.

The first time I saw Schaefer was in the training camp at Augusta, Ga., in the spring of 1907. He impressed me as a jolly, happy-go-lucky, fun-loving German. This impression remained with me for a few weeks and then, one day, I called a meeting of the players to discuss plans for the exhibition tour that would take us back north. In the meeting Schaefer talked much and I discovered that this man who had been clowning for two weeks, playing practical jokes, telling funny stories and who never seemed to have a serious thought, was really a player of

Schaefer and Sam Crawford (*above*) were teammates for five seasons.

marked intellect. He knew baseball and he knew it well. He had plenty of ideas and, unlike a great many ideas carried by ball players, those of Schaefer were sound and workable. He convinced me that he was going to be a strong cog in the wheel and I was not wrong. He proved all of that later.

The more I saw of Schaefer after that, the more I was amazed at his knowledge of the game. His frequent flashes were the more astounding because of his clowning. He would do something extremely foolish or ridiculous and a moment later say something exceedingly wise.

We had a hard fight to win the American League pennant in 1907 and I don't know what we would have done without Schaefer. I have never in my life seen a man who loved the tight situations better than Schaefer. He gloried in battle. He was happiest in those moments when the result hung in the balance. He reveled in close games. He got few hits compared with other players, but most of his hits came with men on bases and meant runs. Frequently they meant victory. He had nerve at bat and he had nerve in the field. Schaefer was one of those fielders who made errors, but never at critical times. In a pinch he always came up with the ball. There are several players of that type. The explanation is that they get careless and play loosely in loose situations, but when much depends on a fielding chance, they tighten and never miss the play. I have seen many men of that type on the major league infields. . . .

When we started on our last eastern trip in September 1907, we had a fighting chance for the pennant. On the train I happened to pick up a Toledo newspaper. Turning to the sports page I noticed a picture of Hans Wagner. It was an action picture, showing Wagner hitting the ball. I got an idea. Going back to the rear end of the coach where Schaefer was engaged in telling stories, I showed him the picture and remarked: "Schaef, if you copy this style at bat and swing on a ball as Wagner does, I'll bet you a suit of clothes that you'll bat at least .500 on this trip." Schaefer looked at the picture carefully and answered, "You're on. Save your money for that suit."

The thing that Wagner did was to get out in front and on top of the ball. He hit the ball before it could break. That is the secret of good batting, but not many batters can do it consistently.

Schaefer copied the Wagner pose and practiced the Wagner style beginning the next afternoon. We played twelve games in the East, winning eleven of them and cinching the pennant, and it was the terrific hitting of Schaefer that was chiefly responsible for the eleven victories.

Schaefer, the reputed weakling at bat, hit for an average better than .500 on that trip. The photograph turned the trick. Schaefer got the knack of meeting the ball out in front. Pitchers who had found him their "meat" suddenly discovered him to be their poison at bat. They did not understand what had happened and attributed the performances to luck, but I knew. I paid more than $100 for a new suit of clothes for Schaefer and paid it gladly.

After batting better than .500 by the use of a certain method, one would think that the player would adopt the method, but Schaefer did not. He went back to his old habits and the next season he was his usual old self at bat, but for two weeks Schaefer was the terror of all pitchers and those two weeks gave Detroit a championship.

On the trip I refer to, Detroit played the memorable seventeen-inning, 9-9 tie game with Philadelphia. The important series of the trip, and the most important series of the season as far as that is concerned, came in Philadelphia. On a Friday I started Bill Donovan, then in his prime and our star pitcher. Schaefer drove in three runs and scored two himself. We won, 5-3.

It rained on Saturday and so a doubleheader was scheduled for the following Monday, baseball being prohibited in Philadelphia on Sunday. We started play at 1:45 on Monday with Donovan again in the box, and there followed what, in my opinion, is the most remarkable game ever played. It went seventeen innings and was called at the end of the seventeenth with the score a tie at nine. . . .

During the game there was a disputed decision with the players crowding around the umpires. During the argument Donovan swung on Monte Cross, a shortstop, but out of the lineup that day and coaching at first base. Cross went down in a heap and a policeman rushed over to arrest Donovan. But Schaefer's quick wit saved the situation. Grabbing the policeman he said, "What are you pinchin' him for? He didn't do nothin'. He was the guy that hit him." Schaefer was pointing to [Claude] Rossman, who was having a bad day. The policeman grabbed Rossman and lugged him off the field, poor Rossman not knowing what it was all about. That prevented us from losing. Donovan finished the game and held the Athletics safe. Another pitcher might have done it, but that is doubtful. Donovan was pitching airtight ball at the time. Playing a tie was the break of the pennant race and threw the advantage to us.

Schaefer's happiest and saddest days in baseball came in succession. We were playing Chicago in Chicago and "Doc" White, the famous left-hander of the White Sox, was pitching. Schaefer was on the bench that day, nursing a sore thumb. Late in the game we filled the bases with two out. I asked Schaefer whether he thought he could pinch bat and he said he would. . . .

When I sent Schaefer to bat, he stepped before the grandstand, doffed his cap and announced: "Ladies and gentlemen, permit me to introduce to you Herman Schaefer, premier batsman of the baseball world. He will now step to the plate and give you a brilliant demonstration of his unmatched skill." He hit the first ball White pitched over the fence. He halted at first and yelled, "At the quarter, Schaefer leads by a length!" He slid into second, got up and yelled, "At the half, Schaefer leads by two lengths!" He slid into third, got up, yelled, "At the three-quarter pole, Schaefer leads by seven lengths!" He slid across the plate, got up and announced, "Schaefer wins by a mile!" Again doffing his cap he told the stands, "Ladies and gentlemen, this concludes the afternoon's performance. I thank you one and all. Get your tickets for the concert after the main show." . . .

The next morning, when we arrived in Detroit, we discovered the newspapers carrying page-wide headlines proclaiming the slugging powers of Schaefer. He was hailed a hero. We were playing Cleveland that afternoon and Addie Joss started for Cleveland. Schaefer never could hit Joss because Schaefer was a full swinger and Joss always fooled him with his slow ball, a delivery that was poison for a swinger. When Schaefer came to bat in the first inning he drew a tremendous ovation. He doffed his cap, then took three swings and sat down. But that is not all. This performance was repeated three times during the game. The home run hero of yesterday proved the batting dub of today. It was the saddest day in Schaefer's career. . . .

Herman Schaefer was the first and greatest comedian of them all. None has been his equal either as a humorist or a pantomimist. Schaefer was the Mathewson of comedians—he had everything. As a ball player he was not a first class fielder, nor a first class hitter, nor a first class base-runner, but, as I have said . . . , he was one of the most valuable players of all time, one of the greatest money players the game has produced. He was a fighter, he had the competitive spirit. I have never met a man whom I would sooner have on my ball club in a pinch than Schaefer. He was a lion-hearted hero in the crisis. He never failed.

The followers of baseball remember him as a buffoon. I presume he will always be remembered as that. Study the averages and you will not form a different conclusion, for Schaefer does not rank high there, but as a clown there has never been his peer.

This clowning business is a fine thing for a ball club, especially one that is up in the pennant race. It helps break the strain and it keeps players in the proper frame of mind. It cuts down their worries and refreshes them. For this reason, if for no other, a man like Schaefer is invaluable to a team.

He is dead and gone but his deeds of comedy live after him. I guess they will be recalled for many years and I doubt if the game will see another man possessing so much originality and unadulterated fun. He was great in his own way and lovable. He got the plaudits of the crowds and how he loved them! That was his life.

Schaefer was a born showman. He knew how to reach the heart of the gallery and how to grip it and hold it.

The comedy of Schaefer did not appeal alone to those that knew baseball; its appeal was universal. Several years ago the Giants and the White Sox took Schaefer on a tour of the world. Schaefer did his clowning on the improvised ball fields of Europe and he did what few men have done—he made kings laugh. The King of England had a hearty laugh over Schaefer's antics and so did royal personages in other countries where the teams played.

One of his first memorable stunts came in a Detroit-Cleveland game. It started to rain in the third inning. Detroit was five runs behind in the score with no chance of winning. It was decided to stall and compel the umpires to call the game before the fifth inning, preventing Detroit from losing.

The late "Silk" O'Loughlin was umpiring behind the plate and he did not like the idea of stalling. It made him sore. He told the Detroit players that they were going to see five innings of play even if there was a repetition of the Johnstown flood and the game had to be finished on rafts. But the stalling tactics continued and O'Loughlin, drenched thoroughly and as angry as he ever was in his life, told the Tigers, "You're going to play nine innings now and that's settled."

Then Schaefer came to bat. The fans, huddled in the grandstand, began to laugh. Schaefer turned and asked O'Loughlin what the laughter was about. O'Loughlin did not know. Then the fans roared and Schaefer again turned to O'Loughlin to ask him what it was about. O'Loughlin, who had been suspicious, suddenly pushed Schaefer to one side and then discovered what the commotion was about. Schaefer was using a goatee. As soon as he took his position at bat he adjusted the goatee. He took it off every time he turned to O'Loughlin, but as soon as he faced the pitcher again he readjusted it.

"That gag don't get you under the nice warm showers," bellowed O'Loughlin. "You toss away that goatee and stay in the game. If you don't get rid of them chin whiskers, I'll plaster a fine on you so big that you'll never get through paying it."

But O'Loughlin was wrong. Schaefer did reach the nice warm showers two innings later. The next time he came to bat he wore a pair of hip boots, an oilskin coat, an oilskin hat, carried a bat in one hand and an open umbrella in the other. He had borrowed the boots, hat and coat from the groundskeeper. The umbrella belonged to a spectator.

"You're out of the game," yelled O'Loughlin, forgetting all about his promise of a few innings before to compel Schaefer to play the full nine innings. . . .

The late Jack Sheridan was a victim of one of Schaefer's pranks but it did not happen on the ball field and Sheridan discovered that he had been kidded several months afterward.

In the wet days Joe Cantillon had a saloon in Chicago located on Clark Street and called the Log Cabin. Ball players, wintering in Chicago, used to gather at the Log Cabin on winter evenings. Sheridan, who wintered in Chicago, also frequented the saloon.

One evening Sheridan got tired of standing at the bar and being a bit dizzy from drink, he had decided to retire to the rear of the place. Beyond the bar was a summer kitchen. A rain pipe ran down the wall against which this kitchen had been built and Sheridan placed a chair against the wall and rested his head against the pipe.

Schaefer had followed Sheridan to the summer kitchen and, noticing him dozing against the rain pipe, he went into the garret and found the top of the pipe. Then he bellowed down: "Jack Sheridan your time has come."

Sheridan jumped off the chair, let out a stifled yell and rushed back into the barroom. He roared to the barkeeper: "Quick Tony, a drink. Make it a stiff one and be quick about it."

Tony followed instructions. Jack shook himself a few times, looked around the place and took an inventory of the scene. Nobody paid any attention to him. There was not the slightest suspicion that any one knew what had happened. Satisfied that he must have been dreaming, Sheridan went back and resumed his seat, once more leaning his head against the water pipe at the side of the room.

Schaefer, who had reentered the barroom, kept watching Sheridan. As soon as he was sure Jack was again dozing, he returned to the garret. Once more the voice of Schaefer bellowed down the water pipe: "Jack Sheridan your time has come."

Sheridan jumped out of his chair and rushed into the barroom. But he did not stop this time. He kept right on going, through the barroom, through the front door and down Clark Street. The last the gang in the Log Cabin, who had all come out on the sidewalk to see what he would do, saw of Sheridan he was still running. And they saw him no more that winter.

Spring passed and summer was well on its way. The heat of a July sun was baking the diamond and Sheridan, behind the bat, was having a tough afternoon. Up came Schaefer. Sheridan called the first one a strike. Schaefer thought it was a ball. Schaefer said nothing. The second ball looked wide to Schaefer but Sheridan called it a strike. Schaefer stepped back and bending toward Sheridan's ear yelled: "Jack Sheridan your time has come."

Schaefer started running just in time. Sheridan ran after him, calling him all the names he could think of. He fined Schaefer and he suspended him and he promised like treatment to any ball player that would ever ask him why he was sore at Schaefer or any one who ever in any way mentioned the incident. . . .

The friendship between Schaefer and [Charlie] O'Leary was strange at times. They were inseparable, but occasionally they had quarrels and then they would not speak for days. I was always amused when they had one of their quarrels, for each of them would come to me and inform me that they were no longer on speaking terms. I remember that at one time they did not speak to each other for three days. They would arrive at the ballpark together, practice together, play together, dress in adjoining lockers and leave together. They ate together and slept together, but neither spoke a syllable to the other. And then one day I would be informed by each that they were again on speaking terms.

Schaefer knew many vaudeville actors and one of them taught him the trick of striking a stage blow. This worked on the principle that the hand is quicker than the eye. The swinging fist would strike the palm of the other hand, held against the face of the man who was supposed to be hit. Schaefer practiced this until he had the trick down to perfection. He and O'Leary would stand in front of the hotel in the evening and get into a heated argument. Suddenly Schaefer swung on O'Leary. A loud smack and O'Leary staggered back as if stunned. Then O'Leary would straighten up and the players would give the laugh to the crowd that had gathered to see the fight.

One evening they were getting big crowds and having lots of fun, but they finally tired of it and decided to quit. George Mullin, the pitcher, wanted to go on with the show and Schaefer told him to do it himself. He showed Mullin how the trick was done. Just as Schaefer left, Eddie Killian, another pitcher, appeared and Mullin asked Killian to join him. Killian was unable to get the hang of the thing, so Mullin compromised. He told Killian: "We'll have a row and then you tell me you're goin' to take a sock at me and swing. I'll put my hand up quick and catch the punch."

Killian agreed and eventually they started the row. As soon as the crowd was sufficiently large, Killian threatened Mullin and Mullin dared him to swing. Killian swung. Mullin put up his hand quickly, but Killian's fist crashed against his jaw and Mullin went down in a heap, absolutely knocked out.

Mullin had overlooked one thing. Killian was a left-hander. He had seen the trick worked only by right-handers.

Schaefer retained his wit until the end. One of his last famous "cracks" came during the war when the word "German" and everything pertaining to it was removed from the English language. Someone suggested that Schaefer's nickname of "Germany" would have to be changed. Schaefer himself suggested the substitute. He said: "From now on I'm to be known as 'Liberty' Schaefer."

Compiled from "Rounding Third" syndicated newspaper columns by Hugh Jennings, 1925.

A syndicated column that carried Babe Ruth's name ran in newspapers across the country in the 1920s. Ruth didn't actually write the pieces, though. They were ghostwritten by friends and associates, including Ford Frick and William Slocum.

1925

Babe Ruth

OWNIE CARROLL

This is the story of how a wise manager signed the best young college pitcher in America. I refer to Ty Cobb of Detroit and his latest find— Ownie Carroll, recently of Holy Cross College in Massachusetts. This is the same young man who has been standing batters on their heads for the past four years—not only leading college batters, but some of the best batters in the American and National leagues.

They tell me Carroll won forty-eight games since 1921 and was only beaten twice. One defeat was by the score of 1-0 in sixteen innings. During the same time he had "made monkeys" out of a dozen big league clubs in exhibition games.

You've got to give the boy credit. But don't overlook giving a big share of credit to Cobb who signed the pitcher when he was only a college freshman. And also save a little credit for Jack Barry, famous old Philadelphia shortstop, now baseball coach at Holy Cross.

GEORGE HERMAN (BABE) RUTH

BIG LEAGUE CHEWING GUM

Detroit played an exhibition game against the Worcester boys in 1921, and that one afternoon convinced Cobb that Carroll was "there." Quietly, and without any noise, Cobb signed the kid who was not yet a star even in college ranks. He soon started mowing down the heavy hitters of Yale, Harvard, Princeton, Boston College, Georgetown and other crack teams, and then the big league scouts got busy. Nine of them were on Carroll's trail at one time. They say one National League club offered him a bonus of $50,000 for his signature. But baseball law recognized Cobb's claims and paid compliment to Cobb's judgment and shrewdness by awarding the college star to Detroit.

Carroll is a plain, modest sort of fellow. I watched him at the stadium posing for the movies the first afternoon he was in uniform. Other Yankee players remarked about his nice way of acting. I had a little talk with him and am sorry I can't describe the boy like a real reporter. All I can say is that Carroll pitches right handed, has nice dark blue eyes and talks good sense. In action he seems to have lots of speed and a clever drop ball. A friend of mine happened to drive Carroll and Cobb to the game the first afternoon and told me how he carried along his college baseball duds; a modest roll containing shoes, sox, and a sweatshirt. Nothing chesty about this boy.

"Don't get discouraged," I told Carroll. "The best pitchers in the game get their bumps."

"Well, I expect to get mine," he replied, "and what's more I guess Cobb expects the same." Then he told me something about Cobb which shows the young fellow is certainly going to have every chance in the world. "All you got to do is win us one game out of the first six you pitch." That's what Cobb told Carroll in the dressing room before the game. What could be fairer?

As it turned out he failed to win his first game against the Red Sox at Boston. That's nothing when you remember Walter Johnson himself was taken out of his first game twenty years ago. And other great pitching stars have started off badly due to nervousness, stage fright, over-anxiousness, and some times just the breaks of the game.

I know Cobb is sold on him right now and figures that he'll be ready to step in and take his regular turn in the box. And if he does, look out! All the Tigers need is one more good pitcher to make them real pennant contenders.

The way Cobb got wise to Carroll is an interesting story. Along in 1921, Detroit went to Windsor Locks, near Worcester, for an exhibition game with some club there and Carroll pitched against them.

Here's how Cobb tells the story: "I went up to bat the first time and, of course, I figured it would be easy. The kid put one over for a strike, but I didn't think anything of it. Then he put over another one that cut the corner and that was strike two. I figured the thing had gone far enough, and when the third pitch came sailing up big as a house I dug in and got ready to swing. I swung too—and missed as pretty a hook as I've ever saw. Everyone gave me the razz, and the kid grinned at me as I walked back.

"A little later Bob Veach fanned and then Harry Heilmann. And the next time I was up I fanned again. By that time we were beginning to take a little notice and believe me the kid had everything. In that whole nine innings we got just four hits. Veach fanned three times, I fanned twice and I don't know how many of the rest of the club struck out. But there were a lot of them. That was three years ago—and they say he's been getting better and better. If he has, you can take it from me. He's ready."

That's what Ty has to say—and he ought to know a good pitcher when he sees one. And Bobby Veach, now with the Yankees, agrees with him. So do a lot of other boys who have played against Carroll.

It'll be a big boost for the colleges, too, if he gets away to a good start. Seems as though more and more of the college teams are turning out big leaguers. When I broke in, all the old-timers used to laugh at college players and make fun of them. "Go out somewhere and get some experience," they'd say. But there sure are a lot of them playing today and a lot of them stepped right from college into the big leagues and made good.

Lynwood "Schoolboy" Rowe lived up to the hype that accompanied his 1933 debut. By his second season, he was a twenty-four-game winner. In nearly a decade with the Tigers, he pitched on three World Series teams.

1933

C. E. Parker

SCHOOLBOY

NORFOLK, VA—Baseball is not the only sport represented on the Detroit team, which, with the Giants as playmates, will treat Polo Grounds fans tomorrow to their first sight this year of major league baseball.

A track man will be in the Tiger lineup—one who has traveled the one hundred-yard course in close to ten seconds, has tossed the javelin 190 feet, has put the shot forty-seven feet, eight inches, and has high jumped six feet, one inch.

A golfer of ability will be with Bucky Harris's team—one who thinks nothing of driving the pellet 300 to 350 yards and who won an inter-scholastic championship when barely fifteen years of age.

A boxer will have a place in the Tiger lineup—one who, first as a light-weight, later as a welterweight and then as a light heavyweight, laid low a score of adversaries.

A jumping center from the realm

Schoolboy Rowe

39

of basketball will be out there—one who was thrice awarded all-scholastic honors in his state and who was propositioned by numerous colleges when a mere high school sophomore.

A tennis player will take the field against Bill Terry's men—one who won interscholastic championships in that activity and who had the build and the equipment of strokes to become the successor of Bill Tilden.

And a football player of phenomenal skill will participate in tomorrow's exhibition game—one who was employed as an end on defense because of his keenness in diagnosing plays and the finality of his bruising tackle; was used as a back on offense because of his speed, weight, shiftiness and amazing ability at tossing forward passes; led his school team to three state championships, and whose services were sought by South California and many other institutions which specialize in the gridiron pastime.

Reading from left to right or, for that matter, reading from right to left, east to west or north to south, beginning, of course, with the front Rowe, the foregoing may be identified as:

Track star, Lynwood Rowe; golfer, Lynwood Rowe; boxer, Lynwood Rowe; basketball center, Lynwood Rowe; tennis player, Lynwood Rowe; football end, back, and forward pass specialist, Lynwood Rowe.

And, according to the latest word from Bucky Harris, Detroit's starting pitcher tomorrow night will be Lynwood Rowe. And unless he falls down in this department for the first time in his career, the feature batsman of the fray will be—perhaps you've guessed it—Lynwood Rowe.

Schoolboy Rowe, they call him. And folks are saying he is the answer to the constantly recurring question, "What will baseball do for a blazing spot of color when Babe Ruth retires?"

Your agent shares the opinion that if there is a new Ruthian figure on the horizon Schoolboy Rowe is the feller. Indeed, it would not surprise me should Schoolboy, who stretches skyward six feet, four and a half inches, weighs 206 pounds and is barely twenty years old, may begin forthwith to steal the spotlight from the Bambino.

Schoolboy saw his first professional team five years ago. It was the Shreveport, La., outfit, and the youngster, then only fifteen and playing with a kid team, struck out twelve of its batsmen to win the engagement, 5-2.

Schoolboy saw his first professional service last year when he joined the staff of the Beaumont club of the Texas League, at nineteen years of age. And he rang up nineteen victories in twenty-six games while helping his team capture the league title.

Schoolboy saw his first major league team this spring when he joined the Tigers and was tossed against his first major league opposition during the current barnstorming trip of the Tigers and Giants—and he downed the Terrymen twice in as many starts and so comes here tomorrow intent on claiming his third consecutive victory over the New York National League team.

Yet, remarkable as is Schoolboy's pitching record, it may be his wily and wicked wielding of the willow that will make him the Bambino of the not distant future.

Five years ago at Shreveport it was Schoolboy's home run with the bases loaded that clinched the victory in his debut against a professional team. Last year it was eleven home runs by Schoolboy, several of them made with men on, that aided and added to his Beaumont conquests. And he has cuffed a terrific homer in each of his recent games with the Giants.

Had a certain Miss Blackman, who later became Mrs. Travis Jackson, known as much about baseball as she probably has learned since she married the Giants' captain, Schoolboy might be appearing tomorrow in a New York uniform. The present Mrs. Jackson was Schoolboy's school teacher in the grammar grades at Eldorado, Ark. As matters developed, however, Eddie Goosetree, Detroit scout, became the official discoverer of that young man.

Eddie, speaking of the matter the other day, told me he thought he had been given a bum steer when he called at the Rowe domicile in Eldorado to inquire about a kid by that name. A pint-sized little codger who had once been a trapeze performer with Barnum & Bailey's circus answered the bell and said he was Schoolboy's dad. Eddie just couldn't figure how the offspring of such a runty sire could merit big league consideration.

He was informed that Schoolboy, who is still as then he was, more or less a nut on fires, could be located at the engine house. So Eddie went there to complete his disillusionment and found it wasn't to be completed. In fact, it was on the running board of the fire wagon, with the curled-up hose serving as a desk, that the first papers on Schoolboy were signed.

Not a dime was passed to obtain that first signature, and, even when the first option expired and a somewhat wiser Schoolboy demanded an honorarium for its renewal, a mere $500 was all it cost Detroit to obtain the youth who, if he lives up to expectations, will draw hundreds of thousands to the ballparks.

Reprinted from the New York World-Telegram, *April 8, 1933.*

Female reporters were far from common at newspapers in the 1930s, and they were almost unheard of on the sports beat. But the city was so stricken with baseball fever in 1934 that the Detroit Times *enlisted women's columnist Vera Brown to add a different slant to the paper's coverage of the World Series—the first to feature the Tigers in a quarter century. The Cardinals would defeat the hometown heroes in seven games.*

1934

Vera Brown

YEARNING FOR DETROIT

ST. LOUIS, MO— Here we are five hundred miles from home and I wish somebody would send a wire saying: "Come home, all is forgiven."

Personally I'm hanging on the ropes. Not because of yesterday's defeat at Sportsman's Park at the hands of another Dean in the third game of the World Series. But just because of the cheering—or lack of it!

Mike Cochrane is still smiling. We'll be back in Detroit for that sixth game on Monday. But the folks down here forget what voices are for and I'm lonesome for a good old-fashioned baseball audience, which knows how to yell.

Chief Hogsett

When that nine-inning game ended yesterday with the defeat of our Tigers, the crowd, which was not quite capacity, melted quickly. All during the game they did not seem to have the proper enthusiasm for 42,000 fans who were seeing their team win. When the counting was over I climbed down some millions of stairs from the press box to the street in search of a taxi. I came out on Spring

Avenue. There was no taxi, but there were a lot of people waiting for some kind of conveyance.

Suddenly out of the exit to the ballpark appeared a familiar tall figure. It was "Daf," one-half of the Dean Bros., Paul "Daffy" Dean, who had pitched the Cardinals to victory. Behind him came Frankie Frisch, manager of the Cardinals. Somebody standing beside me remarked: "There's Frisch and Daffy!"

People stared. Daffy and Frisch walked over into the parking lot unmolested and got into a waiting car. "Daf" was carrying some fan mail. Nobody asked for an autograph. Nobody yelled. I could not believe it. If it had been Detroit—Schoolboy Rowe and Mike Cochrane—there would have been a small-sized blot! Some of the girls dared to turn their heads and remark that Daffy is better looking than Dizzy Dean, his brother. That settled the matter so far as the St. Louis fans were concerned. Now you know why I want to come home.

If the home folks are disappointed, just try talking to any one of the Tigers today. They can't forgive themselves for yesterday's defeat.

Hank Greenberg was so upset he refused to eat any dinner. That beautiful three-base hit he got in the ninth inning, which wrecked Daffy's hope for a shutout, was small consolation to him.

There were a lot of Tiger men on bases during the game and Hank failed to come through. Goose Goslin did some nice hitting, so did a lot of the boys, but not when we had men piled up ready to score.

If you are doing any reviling, remember that the boys of the Tiger team are doing more. But they say today they'll "take the Cards."

The Dean Brothers have an evil eye on the Detroiters. There are four more games to go, and the Tigers have no fear for the final result.

Scores of the famous and near-famous crowded the park here yesterday. The fans from Hollywood and New York who were in Detroit followed the Tigers and the Cardinals into the Cards' hometown. Walter O. Briggs was here sitting next to Mr. and Mrs. Frank J. Navin over by the Tiger dugout.

St. Louis had more fans in the ballpark last Sunday for the game which won the pennant for their team than they did yesterday in the World Series game. For this town just knows the hard-hitting Cardinals will win. People down here say Schoolboy Rowe's victory on Thursday was just a fluke. That is, those fans who did not see that superb game say it.

That game gave the Cardinals a healthy respect for our Tigers, however.

The Schoolboy today is anxious to get back to pitch again. The weather down here is warm, almost hot. It is the kind of weather the Schoolboy loves.

As he waited on the bench yesterday, he was presented to the governor of Missouri and the mayor of St. Louis. They all wanted to meet the formidable pitcher from Arkansas.

Ticket scalpers are working overtime here, but to no purpose. Yesterday they could not unload their tickets before the game. After it was over they were trying to buy up tickets for today's game. Those vacant seats in the pavilions wrecked their plans. Their only hope is for big business Sunday.

Fur coats have disappeared down here. We're almost ready to call our summer hats back again. Edna Mary Skinner's sister, Audrey, joined her here from Eldorado for today's game. Miss Edna Mary Skinner is the fiancée of the Schoolboy.

"I had to sit up all night on the train up from home," Miss Audrey said. "There were so many fans aboard that there were not enough Pullmans and I did not try to make a reservation early.

"You know, everybody keeps asking me questions about the Schoolboy. Well, I know him hardly at all for he has been away from home ever since I've been grown up."

Miss Audrey is only eighteen.

"One man I want to meet on the Tiger team is Hank Greenberg," she added.

Right then and there in the lobby of the Kingsway Hotel, Audrey met Hank. And another fan was added to Hank's long list.

Mickey and Mrs. Cochrane went out last night for a quiet dinner with Mr. and Mrs. Al Simmons. Simmons is a White Sox outfielder, and a great one.

Mickey is still limping, but he'll be in today's game with his jaw set. If the Tigers come off with the championship, it will be Mickey's victory. It is his determination that is keeping his team going. Some of the Tigers went to the first show at the movies last night and came home by 10, ready for bed. They like to sit quietly through an early movie after a hard game. It relaxes them and they sleep better.

"Just have faith in us," said Marvin Owen, the Tigers' third baseman. "We'll come through. You trusted us all season. Give us a little more faith now!"

The Dean family was jubilant last night. But there was one fly in the intoxicating ointment of their victory. They had not "shut the door in the Tigers' faces" as they promised. Hank Greenberg, the man of whom Dizzy said he was not afraid, got a home run off Dizzy up in Detroit on Wednesday and it was Hank who yesterday hit Jo-Jo White home for the Tigers' only run with a three-base slug. So there was not a row of goose eggs in the Tiger score, as "Daf" had hoped there would be.

Dizzy got the only ovation of the day yesterday.

Pepper Martin, third baseman, came in for his share when the fans got enough pep to yell, but when Dizzy came out in the eighth and began warming up they applauded him. Pepper, by the way, is a veteran of the 1931 World Series in which the Cardinals played.

Bleachers and grandstands spread around the entire diamond here in St. Louis and make the park seem smaller than it is.

The only spot for all the photographers, movie and still men, is on top of the pavilions, and there are no railings about the roof. They perch on the edge of the roof and worry spectators who expect them to fall off at a crucial moment. When a fly ball hits on the roof of the pavilions the patter of photographers' feet drowns out every other sound up in the press box. The whole place shakes. Those boys of the cameras were not above scrambling for souvenir balls, I can tell you. They got several yesterday.

Mrs. Elon C. Hogsett said today she was proud of her husband. He pitched a fine game against the Cards after Tommy Bridges was knocked out of the box. "The Chief," and by the way he is not an Indian at all, allowed the Cards only one hit and that did not mean anything.

"I held them the first day, too," remarked the Chief quietly. "I'm not afraid of them. They are nothing to scare us. Watch our smoke the next two days!"

The Chief is a silent bronzed lad who worked in the oil fields of Oklahoma in his early days and knows one-eyed Wiley Post of Oklahoma of round-the-world fame.

"I guess people think everybody who has lived in Oklahoma is an Indian if he has black hair," says the Chief.

"The Chief" is a nice nickname. Hogsett does not mind. He does not mind the war whoops with which his appearance is always greeted. He just begins that beautiful, and for a while baffling, delivery of his and lets them yell.

Mrs. Patricia Dean, wife of the pitching Dizzy, put her silver fox furs about her shoulders in triumph last night as the game ended.

"Didn't I tell you the Dean Brothers were wonderful!" she cried. "They are beyond anything you can imagine. Just you wait until you see 'Dizz' in another game or two when he is right. It will be something to watch. He can pitch a couple of games if he wants to get in this series."

Dizz goes on a ten-week vaudeville tour when the season closes. His vacation will be just a few short weeks in his Florida home before spring training, Mrs. Dean says.

John Klem, veteran umpire of seventeen World Series, oldest umpire in the National League in point of service, worked at home plate yesterday and the fans had him furious. They kept yelling at him: "Catfish! Catfish!" The more angry he got, the more the fans yelled.

Just why the fans call Klem "Catfish" remains somewhat of a mystery. He is a dignified person. And he did not like that "Catfish" business. Will Rogers got a great kick out of Klem's rage and Joe E. Brown and George Raft added their voices to those of the harassing fans.

Reprinted from the Detroit Times, *October 6, 1934.*

It was the defeat of the Tigers in the 1934 World Series that made the 1935 victory so glorious and celebrated. The Tigers lost to St. Louis after being up three games to two. The final contest, which the Cardinals won 11-0, included a raucous near-riot by fans after a spiking incident involving Joe Medwick. This game report spotlights a Detroit victory in game four. Damon Runyon, the author, was famous at the time, his stories having been made into movies and, later, the stage hit Guys and Dolls.

1934

Damon Runyon

GAME FOUR

SPORTSMAN'S PARK, ST. LOUIS—Detroit 10, St. Louis 4. Thus ends the fourth game of the World Series of 1934.

This result ties the series between the American and National league champions at two-all.

Detroit humiliated big, gawky-looking Hank Greenberg, the young Jewish giant from New York's Bronx, this afternoon by dropping him down in the Tigers' batting order from fourth, the "clean-up" position, to sixth.

The "clean-up" position is a high compliment to a man's batting ability. It has the same importance in a baseball batting order as the headliner's spot in vaudeville. The "clean-up" man feels he is somebody. Sixth place is demotion—a reduction in the ranks.

The dropping down of big Hank Greenberg, not so long ago the pride of James Monroe High School, is due to Hank's

Elden Auker

48

previous batting inefficiency in the World Series. He had been standing at the plate, bare-armed and burly, twiddling his bat in huge fingers as the pitchers slipped the ball past him greased with their various magic.

A figure of futility. So down he goes in the batting order. Big Hank's pride is sorely wounded. He has been insulted, degraded.

So he picks up his bat this afternoon and bludgeons out four safe hits, including two tremendous doubles, knocking in the winning run for the Detroit Tigers in the seventh inning, besides making a remarkable one-handed stop of a smash from "Pepper" Martin's bat in the sixth when the score is tied. The stop smothers a certain two-bagger.

Thereafter the Tigers get five more runs in the eighth, but the important tally remains the one pushed in by big Hank, playing his first season in the big league at the age of twenty-three.

He stands six feet four inches and weighs 215 pounds and when he slams a baseball it travels high and far. The trouble with Hank up to today has been that he had not been slamming the ball. As a matter of fact, all the Tigers hit today behind the steady pitching of Elden Auker, a right-hander with a quick underhand delivery that seems to bring the baseball up from down around his shoe tops.

They pound "Tex" Carleton, old "Dazzy" Vance, Willie Walker, Jess Haines and Jim Mooney for a total of thirteen hits, while Auker is keeping the Cardinals' ten hits pretty well scattered out across the nine innings.

It is an old-fashioned, town-lot sort of baseball game, with everything happening, and it keeps the 37,492 spectators interested, even though many of them are annoyed with the Cardinals at the finish. The result should delight the Detroit hotelkeepers, anyway, as the series is now certain to go back there for at least one more game.

Even the redoubtable "Dizzy" Dean gets into the game, being put in by manager Frankie Frisch to run the bases in place of Virgil Davis, a successful pinch-hitter in the fourth, when the Cardinals tie the score.

Dean is hit on the head by a thrown ball, knocked down and has to be carried off the field by his teammates, but his head figured in the scoring just the same.

This incident occurs after Ernie Orsatti singles, and Leo Durocher is safe on Gehringer's error. Davis singles, scoring Orsatti and putting Durocher on third. Then "Dizzy" goes in to run for Davis, a strange and risky role for a million dollar pitcher. Martin hits to Gehringer and Gehringer tosses to Rogell, covering second, for a force play on Dean.

Then Rogell starts a throw to first to double up Martin and the galloping "Dizzy" somehow gets his noodle in the way of the throw. As a matter of fact, it looks as if he leaps into the air, apparently with some idea of interfering with the throw. The ball hits him on the head, and down he goes. Meantime, Durocher is scoring with the tying tally.

There is great excitement as "Dizzy" is carried off by his comrades, who handle him as gently as if he is a sack of eggs. Later comes the report that he will pitch tomorrow, although he went to a hospital to see if the blow jarred anything inside his bean.

It is said Cochrane may pitch Bridges against Dean, though the logical, sensible choice would seem to be Rowe. Tomorrow's is the game to win, with the series tied.

The Cards' five errors make a total of nineteen misplays for the two clubs in four games, possibly some new sort of record. The Tigers' eleven men left on bases today brings their total in this respect up to forty-three, surely another new mark for four World Series games.

Reprinted from a syndicated newspaper column by
Damon Runyon, 1934.

Detroit baseball fans are some of the most passionate—and certainly not shy about sharing their thoughts and wisdom, as illustrated by this note to Mickey Cochrane. The letter reached the Tigers manager the day after his team had opened the 1935 World Series with a 3-0 loss to the Cubs. Detroit rallied to take four of the next five games, capturing the championship.

1935

"A Bunch of Tigers Fans"

ADVICE FOR THE MANAGER

Dear Mike,

The best defense is a good offense.

Why not put [Gee] Walker in center field and get that batting power in the lineup where it belongs?

Would the story have been different yesterday had [Pete] Fox led off in the first inning with that hit of his? It sure would have been more inspiring than that strikeout of [Jo-Jo] White's. Then when Hank [Greenberg] and Goose [Goslin] got those walks, it sure would have raised your hopes if Walker was coming up to bat, 'cause you must admit that the boy hits 'em when they are needed.

Certainly the Cub pitchers are not worried about White leading the batting order (they have only to look at his batting average to know that if they pitch to him it is a sure out). Imagine the difference they notice when they start off with Fox leading the batting order. Not a weak spot all

DETROIT	1	2
9 FOX Right Field		
3 COCHRANE Catcher		
2 GEHRINGER Second Base		
5 GREENB'RG First Base		
4 GOSLIN Left Field		
7 ROGELL Short Stop		
6 WALKER Center Field		
8 OWEN Third Base		
Pitcher		

the way down the list to the tail end. It certainly can give your opposing pitcher more worry than he has with your present lineup.

In the subject of conversation among Detroit fans some accuse you of being personally "down" on Walker, while White is a sort of "teacher's pet" under your wing. No one but yourself knows the reasons why, so use that good judgment of yours and make the right fair decision about the matter.

While Joe Sullivan is credited with pulling the team out of the early slump last spring, how about Walker? Walker played in every game and was batting like a madman. Certainly he furnished some of the inspiration to his mates with his good hitting. But, alas, the Detroit sports writers (so-called) if they do not like a player will ride him forever and woe to him that they start to make the goat.

Even with his shortcoming of "being caught off base," Walker gets on base, which is more than some of the other players on the team seem able to do.

What do you think Walker would be hitting if he was batting number four? Here is a guess that the boy would be doing his stuff and be right there where Hank is, perhaps knocking runs in when they are really needed. Somehow Hank seems to knock in runs just in the games that the Tigers lead by a large margin. But in a close game that could be won by one or two runs, Walker has been the boy to knock them in.

Think it over, Mickey, and give the boy a break. What say?

Best of luck for today!
A Bunch of Tigers Fans

Excerpted from Baseball: The Fan's Game *by Mickey Cochrane, published in 1939.*

The world's eyes were on Detroit in 1935, when after decades of trying the Tigers finally won a world championship. Renowned syndicated sports writer Grantland Rice captured the atmosphere in this piece.

1935

Grantland Rice

VICTORY FINALLY

The Leaning Tower can now crumble and find its level with the Pisan plain. The Hanging Gardens can grow up in weeds. After waiting forty-eight years, the Detroit Tigers at last are baseball champions of the world. Nothing else matters in this mad, delirious city.

Let time's ancient bough shed decaying worlds as the rattle of machine guns echoes along Ethiopian trails. This makes no difference at all in the city that waited and won at last—from the dynasty of Hughie Jennings, Ty Cobb, Sam Crawford and Wild Bill Donovan to the title-winning punch that Goose Goslin fired in the ninth as Mickey Cochrane delivered the big run in person.

As the series count stood four and two in favor of the Tigers, over 48,000 Detroit fans opened up a vocalistic cataclysm that is still sweeping Michigan. And above all the rack and the roar there came

Goose Goslin

53

one remembered chant—"Go tell the cock-eyed world, the Old Gray Goose ain't dead."

It was the Old Gray Goose—Goose Goslin, working in partnership with Mickey Cochrane—that finally beat back the last wild charge of Charlie Grimm's game young Cubs.

And you can write it down in your book that these same Cubs were clawing and scratching and snarling and biting up to the final play as Tommy Bridges, the Tennessee rifleman, and Larry French, the Chicago southpaw, fought it out on even terms, blow for blow, until Cochrane's third hit put him in position to ride home on the line smash to center from the old Jersey marsh hunter who was helping to win pennants and World Series over ten years ago.

The Tigers figured to win this championship on experience and the old-fashioned batting eye.

The dope worked out, even with Hank Greenberg, their main cannoneer, nursing a swollen arm through the last four games.

But Cochrane's scrambled infield, with its depleted batting strength, held together, with [Flea] Clifton and [Marv] Owen handling the defensive side ably all along the scrappy route.

In checking back, you will find that 286,672 fans paid in or paid out slightly more than a million dollars to see these six games that were full of snarls and mistakes, but also full of flame and action—most of them fought and decided down the stretch where any slight turn might have marked a new series map.

Before going any further, it might be just as well to pause at this spot and hang a chaplet of wild-apple blossoms around the slender neck of Tommy Bridges, the Tiger pitcher.

The Cubs had been raking him fore and aft, here and there, up and down, most of the afternoon. It was not Bridges on one of his big days. It was an afternoon of trouble from the second inning on. Bridges was in more holes than an army corps of moles. But he kept working his way out from the valley to the upland, from defeat to another chance.

But Bridges reserved the main repertory for the big climax in the ninth.

Get the picture. The score was tied at 3-3. The Cubs had spiked him for eleven hits. It was quite apparent that one run meant the ball game and possibly the championship. At this ticklish moment, Stan Hack kicked in with a low liner that cleared Gerald Walker's head for a triple. Here was a Cub on third, only a few steps from a run that looked taller than Mt. Everest. And there was nobody out. It was ten to one on a seventh game, with the series tied up. In the face of this emergency, Tennessee Tommy struck out [Bill] Jurges, threw out Larry French and collared Augie Galan on a fly to left.

This was the big spot of the closing day. It was a big third act that paved the way for the dramatic finish, when Cochrane singled and the Old Gray Goose plastered a line hit over second that left some fifty thousand spectators from pit to top gallery in the midst of an epileptic epilogue that might seem incredible if you were not there.

After a brief sporting span of some twenty-five years, that jungle-throated roar from forty-eight thousand human throats as Goslin singled and Cochrane scored is one of the reverberations I won't forget. It was the pent up vocal outbreak of nearly fifty years and it exploded with the suppressed power of nitroglycerine when the big moment came.

The young Chicago Cubs, with their run of twenty-one straight, with their victories over the Deans and the Cardinals, just missed the punch and the experience that might have carried them through. They had to fall back on the buggy-whip arm of Lon Warneke, the world champion tobacco chewer from Mt. Ida, Ark., who held the Tigers run-less in his two starting games. It was Lon Warneke who rang down the curtain on Eldorado and Schoolboy Rowe, but Warneke had to work alone. [Charlie] Root, [Thornton] Lee and French lacked the stuff needed to put the silencer on Tiger bats.

It remained for Tommy Bridges to win the two vital games, where only one of the stoutest hearts in competition saved him at the last jump, when Cub fans were at his throat.

Just two years ago Mickey Cochrane came from Philadelphia to Detroit. In his first season, the triple-threat football player from Boston University won the first pennant Detroit had known in twenty-five years, dating back to 1909, when Cobb and Crawford were in their prime.

In his second Tiger season he won the pennant again—but this time the main offensive threat was on its way up the hill. With his leading artilleryman out of action, Greenberg, a leader in home runs and runs driven in, Cochrane reorganized his force and broke the spell of forty-eight years with a ball club that hung on and still kept shooting.

More than one or two things have happened in the last forty-eight years. But so far as Detroit is concerned, the big story of this period was written Monday afternoon when the Tiger manager stepped on home plate and said to the baseball world—"Here it is!"

Mickey Cochrane, the star catcher and manager who brought the Tigers their first championship, nearly died when hit in the skull by a pitched baseball. At the time batters did not wear helmets. Though he returned to manage the Tigers, Cochrane was never the same man, said friends. Joe Williams of the New York World-Telegram *visited Cochrane in the hospital after the mishap and filed this poignant story.*

1937

Joe Williams

MICKEY'S DONE

DETROIT—I called on Mickey Cochrane at the Henry Ford Hospital here today, and in the first interview he has had with a newspaper man since a thrown ball by Bump Hadley of the New York Yankees fractured his skull in three places a month ago, he told me he was through with baseball.

"I'll never catch another game," said the black-haired manager of the Detroit Tigers. "As a player I'm through for all time. Whether I'll continue as a manager I can't say. I'm not thinking about my baseball future these days. All I'm thinking about is getting well."

Cochrane is still a very sick man, though definitely on his way to complete recovery. I was permitted to see him for only a brief interval. His visitors are restricted to three a day. A nurse is constantly in attendance. She regulates the time visitors may stay in the sick chamber.

The one-time fiery leader of the Tigers, distinguished for his aggressive spirit and brilliant play on the ball field, lay stretched out

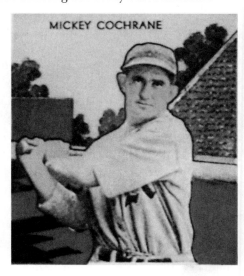

MICKEY COCHRANE

full length in his bed when I called. He lay with the right side of his head cushioned deep in a pillow, held tightly in his right hand. There were no visible marks of the injury that brought him to the threshold of death. Only his deep-set, sunken eyes mirrored the acute pain he had suffered—still suffers, in fact.

"Most days I feel pretty good," he said, "and on others I feel awful. The pain comes and goes. And the steady confinement gets me down. I've been on my back for four weeks now. Haven't been able even to sit up. They X-rayed my head again yesterday and the plates show the fractures are healing. I may get out in two weeks. Or it may be a month. It's hard to say."

When Cochrane does get out, it will take him some time to regain the use of his legs. "I don't suppose I could take five steps now without falling on my pan." He keeps thrashing his legs under the white sheets as if to stimulate circulation. He says when he gets out he is going to some quiet mountain resort to build himself up. He'd like to go to the Wyoming ranch, where he went last year to recuperate from a nervous collapse. "But the docs say I wouldn't be able to stand such a long trip, so I don't know just where I'll go."

Talking about the ball which felled him, Cochrane repeated he lost it in the sun. "I was probably a little careless at the plate, too. The count was three and one and I was prepared to take the next pitch, no matter whether it was over or not. So I was standing at the plate relaxed, knowing I wasn't going to swing anyway and maybe I wasn't as alert as I might have been, say, if the count had been three and two or two and two, with the possibility of the next pitch being a strike."

Cochrane absolved Hadley of all blame. "He's not the type of man who would throw at a batter's head, and besides, why would any pitcher try to bean a hitter with the count three and one?" It was news to Cochrane that Hadley had called to see him at the New York hospital. "I don't remember anything about the first three or four days I was in the hospital. For a long time I guess my mind was in what the boys call a transom." He smiled weakly.

I asked Cochrane if he thought the hitters should be compelled to wear some sort of head protection. "Absolutely," he answered. "A thrown ball even in the hands of a careful, sporting pitcher can perform weird tricks on the way to the plate, and a hitter is liable to be struck any time." Cochrane pressed the pillow against his throbbing head. "I certainly wish I had worn a helmet or something that day at Yankee Stadium."

Cochrane knew I had just come from Chicago after seeing the Louis-Braddock fight. He is a confirmed fight addict. At Boston College, where he exposed himself to the shock of a higher education, he boxed as a middleweight. He was interested in first-hand details of the championship.

"I tried to listen to the fight on the radio, but after the first two rounds I had to turn it off. I found myself getting too nervous. When Louis went down in the first round, I almost jumped out of bed." Cochrane didn't know Louis had won until he read the newspapers the next morning. He went to sleep feeling confident the Irishman would win.

I tried to describe the finishing blow, the tremendous power behind it, just where the blow landed, and how Braddock was toppled in his tracks. A faint smile fluttered over the great catcher's features. "Maybe Braddock should have worn a helmet, too, eh?" he answered.

We got around to talking about baseball and his team, now under the direction of Del Baker, his assistant. The Tiger games are broadcast here every day. "I try to listen to the broadcasts but I can't. Two or three innings are about all I can stand. My nerves get jumpy, my head starts to throb, and I have to call it quits. But the fellows are doing pretty well, aren't they?"

He knew they were playing the Yankees today. "I'd like to see them take a couple of those games and come near the top. They can still win the pennant, because the Yankees aren't showing the power or consistency that was expected of them. It's still an open race, and it would be more open if we could get some pitching from Rowe." Cochrane then revealed Schoolboy Rowe, the big fast-baller, is the only one of his players he has seen since he was hurt. "Rowe comes here to the hospital two or three times a week for some sort of treatment, and he drops in for a little talk. I don't know what's wrong with his arm, and neither does he. He hasn't won a game for us this year, and here it is July almost."

I asked Cochrane how close the Tigers came to getting Rollie Hemsley from the Browns as his replacement. Cochrane rates Hemsley as the best catcher in baseball. A couple of years ago he used the St. Louis receiver instead of himself in the All-Star game, explaining he was putting the "strongest possible lineup on the field."

"I don't know how close they came to getting him. I didn't even know they had tried to get him. I haven't been in condition to consider such details, and nobody in the office has attempted to worry me about the affairs of the club. In fact, all I know about the club is what I read in the newspapers."

I had almost overstayed my allotted time as a visitor, and the nurse indicated her concern. I got up to go and mumbled some fatuous remark about tough luck and such. Cochrane screwed his head in the pillow and smiled faintly. "It could have been a whole lot worse. They tell me some of you fellows even had me dead, and that all of you turned out obituaries on me. I hope you sent one to Jimmy Dykes. I know he'd enjoy reading it." Cochrane and Dykes, best of friends, have been feuding good naturedly for years.

As I left the room, Cochrane's soft voice floated up from the rumpled bed coverings. "And when you see [Joe] McCarthy tell him those Yankees of his aren't in that World Series yet."

Though still a desperately sick man, Cochrane manages to hold fast to all his charm, his fine sense of pleasantry and his competitive fire. But the sight of this great ball player, so accustomed to intense activity, lying helpless in a hospital bed, trying gallantly to fight off physical pain and mental despair, leaves you with a sickening feeling in the pit of your stomach. And you know as you step out into the street how hard it was for him to say, "I've caught my last ball game." No ball player ever loved the game more deeply.

Reprinted from the New York World-Telegram, *June 27, 1937.*

Long before Roger Maris topped Babe Ruth's single-season home-run mark, Tiger first baseman Hank Greenberg riveted the nation's attention with a chase of his own. Greenberg's quest took on even greater significance because of his Jewish faith—and Hitler's rise in Germany.

1938

Bob Murphy

CHASING BABE

In this land of the free and home of the brave, the big question today is: "Can he make it?"

There is no shuffle of marching feet, no roar of armored tanks down well-paved streets. There is no rush for gas masks and no whimpering women standing over cradles of their children.

But in Detroit, at least, the question still is: "Can he make it?"

News kids on the corners confide in each other. They know that Hank Greenberg, the towering Bronx buccaneer, yesterday hit two home runs and sent his season's home run total soaring to fifty-eight—just two short of Babe Ruth's record setting pace of sixty in 1927.

HANK GREENBERG, *Tigers*

Yes, the news' kids confide, and hope and pray. Because big Henry Greenberg happens to be just as much of an idol to them as any European dictator is to his subjects. It would be a safe wager to say that more prayers will be uttered from the lips of Detroit's newsboys within the next two days than ever before.

First of all, they love that tall, towering giant from the Bronx. Secondly, his home run exploits sell papers for them.

This writer cornered Greenberg in his hotel room last night. It was shortly before midnight. The big fellow was in red pajamas, all set to call it a day and leave the responsibility of the world to other people.

We talked of his home runs, his chance to break Ruth's record, and the games in which sensational plays kept him from making home runs.

Greenberg, we think, is the most frank, the most sincere, the most businesslike of all ball players. He doesn't want a line of publicity, unless it is deserved. He won't go for it then if you ask him to subscribe to things he doesn't believe in.

"How do you feel about it all?" this writer asked.

Greenberg broke into a wide smile, fidgeted about like a kid.

"You know," he said, "if I never hit another home run the rest of my life, I won't feel badly. I never dreamed I could get this close to Ruth's record.

"It would be great," Hank recalled, "to have all the home runs you lose through breaks of the game or sensational catches. I can think of five robberies of me this season.

"There was the game in New York. Boy, did I paste that one. I hit the left centerfield fence, 430 feet away. This was the hardest hit ball I powdered all season. But I didn't get a home run. My first trip into Cleveland this season I hit one to deep centerfield. Roy Weatherly ran. It seemed to me he ran for miles. He finally stuck his glove up, stumbled as he did, and caught the ball. That was a tough one.

"There was a day in Philadelphia when I hit two against the toughest wind I've ever known. The wind blew both back into the ballpark."

Greenberg went to his desk, produced his own written records, and started to relate a few statistics for us.

"Henry Edwards, the American League secretary, almost jinxed me," said Greenberg. "Edwards on August 7 sent me a copy of all the home runs I had made up to date. He included a copy of Babe Ruth's homers. At that time I had only thirty-eight home runs. I told him I needed only twenty-two to tie, and it was a swell time to be doing a thing like that. Sure enough, he did jinx me for a while. I went from August 7 to August 19 without hitting a home run."

Hank then started counting his home runs, at the same time comparing his record with Ruth's.

The year Babe hit sixty he clouted them in his specially built park at Yankee Stadium and the other thirty on the road.

Up to now, Hank has hit nineteen on the road and thirty-nine at home.

If you are a demon for statistics, his record shows that on the road he has hit three home runs against Chicago, Cleveland and Boston. He blasted four against New York and two against Washington. Three were made against Philadelphia and only one against St. Louis.

At home, Hank has made seven each against St. Louis, Chicago, New York and Philadelphia. He added six against Washington pitchers and three against Boston pitchers.

Incidentally, when Greenberg hit two home runs yesterday, it marked the eleventh game this season where he has walloped two.

You inquire of Hank if he figures he must break the record against St. Louis here in the next two days. He replies calmly: "I'd like to. But I've hit three in Cleveland already this season. I might get hold of one there, too."

Hank fears photographers now more than he does rival pitchers.

"I'll never complain," he said, "because it's better to have them taking your pictures than not taking them. But I dread to think what I'm going to have to face every time I go to bat the rest of the way out."

Reprinted from the Detroit Times, *September 28, 1938.*

Bobo Newsom, with a 21-5 record, played an integral role in helping the 1940 Tigers win the American League pennant. A spirited character who would change teams thirteen times in his twenty-year career, Newsom allowed fewer than 1.4 runs per game in the World Series, but Cincinnati won in seven games. The match-up had much greater personal significance for Newsom.

1940

Edgar Hayes

ONE FOR DAD

CINCINNATI, OCT. 3—Death today cast a pall of sorrow over the whole Detroit Tiger World Series delegation. Henry Quellin Buffkin Newsom, sixty-eight, father of Buck, died in the hotel here at 6 A.M. A heart attack, the second he suffered during the night, caused his death.

The elder Newsom came to Cincinnati to see his son pitch in the first game of the World Series. It was the second time he had ever seen Buck in the major leagues. He had suffered a serious heart attack during the summer and Buck paid a hurried visit to his home in Hartsville, S.C., at the time.

While in South Carolina Buck promised his father if he were well enough he would bring him north to see the World Series. He assured his father at that time he would be pitching in the series.

His father, buoyed by his son's promise, recovered enough to plan the trip. At the time he left home for

Buck Newsom

63

the game he told his family: "Nothing will keep me from seeing Buck in the World Series. He kept his end of the bargain. Now I will keep mine, even if I don't return."

He sat in a second deck seat and climbed a long stairs to reach it. Buck was arranging a box seat for him today. He saw his son send the Tigers away to a flying start in the 1940 World Series. He watched as the crowd turned from hostile to a keen appreciation of a fine pitcher giving a grand exhibition of his art.

After the game Buck told all the newspapermen about his dad being present. He got a great kick out of giving the gentleman's full name, Henry Quellin Buffkin. He painstakingly spelled it out for each newcomer.

When Bruce Campbell gave him the ball that ended the game, Buck presented it to manager Del Baker. Baker kissed the ball and returned it to the hurler. Buck thanked his boss and said: "This will go back to Hartsville with dad when he goes after the series."

Buck and the other members of the family found the lobby and dining rooms of the Netherland Plaza Hotel too crowded, so they ordered their dinner in the room to avoid the excitement they knew their presence would stir.

Shortly after dinner Mr. Newsom was seized with a heart attack. His whole family gathered in his room and spent practically the entire night. Just about dawn the second attack occurred and he passed away.

Funeral services will be held here this afternoon for members of the family and friends. Later in the night the body will be returned to Hartsville. Buck will leave after the services for Detroit to rejoin the Tigers in the world championship series. Manager Baker left the decision whether to stay with the team or return home to Buck, and he decided to carry on.

Reprinted from the Detroit Times, *October 3, 1940.*

Many Negro League observers thought Satchel Paige more likely than Jackie Robinson to break the major league color barrier. When he pitched at Briggs Stadium in September 1941, Paige sparked thoughts of such possibilities. This story, as you will discover from its tone, comes from a source rarely tapped for sports anthologies: the Daily Worker, *the organ of the American Communist Party. It would be another six seasons before the Dodgers fielded Jackie Robinson—and ten after that before the Tigers integrated.*

1941

William Allan

SATCHEL IN THE PARK

He came, he pitched, he conquered, both the Chicago Negro Giants and the vast throng of 34,784 fans who made the ballpark ring at Briggs Stadium with cheer after cheer for the greatest pitcher they had seen in Detroit in many a day. Who else could it be but the immortal Satchel Paige, whose feats of baseball pitching are legendary?

The great Negro pitcher pitched the first game of a double-header between his team, the Kansas City Monarchs, and the Chicago Negro Giants to one of the greatest crowds the Tigers' ball yard has seen since the World Series. . . .

Effortless, superb, strike after strike rolled across the plate as batter after batter watched them go by with bat still on shoulder as the signboard flashed out three strikes on the batter.

At the beginning of the seventh inning, only one man had gotten to second base. . . . By that time Satchel's great pitching and the excellent support from his teammates had rolled up an 11-run lead.

Briggs Stadium

Then one or two hits slipped through. But any time that a rally threatened for the Chicago team that great whip-like arm went into action and the rally vanished like one of the puffs of dust on the diamond.

The Kansas City Monarchs, whom Paige was pitching for, won both ends of a double-header. . . .

Paige went the whole way in the first game, gave six hits and did not allow a run until the seventh. He fanned four, walked one.

Tiger owner Walter Briggs, sitting in one of the field boxes, must have known, just as he probably has known for a long time, how the Detroit baseball fans feel about Negro players and the keen desire of Detroiters to see such remarkable pitching in the staggering Detroit Tigers. White workers, side by side with their Negro brothers from the assembly lines and factories of Detroit, gave ovation after ovation to the great Satchel as he walked off the mound inning after inning with batters "feeling only the wind of the fireball," as one worker sitting beside us remarked.

Outstanding support was given Satchel, particularly by two of his teammates. First baseman [Buck] O'Neil, whose fishing of them out of the air was breath-taking . . . , brought the house down. Sluggers there were aplenty. Outstanding was outfielder Ted Strong. Strong had a triple and two doubles and displayed a throwing arm, the equal of which has not been seen at Briggs Stadium this year. His pegs to home plate and the bases evoked thunderous applause.

"Look at that catcher" came time and again from the seats around us. The catcher was [Lloyd] Bassett from the Chicago Negro Giants, a craftsman if ever we saw one.

In the second game, the Kansas City Monarchs put on a display of pitching, sending in for two or three innings several Negro fireball pitchers that had the Detroit fans whistling and leaping at the blinding speed. Detroit sure could, with their limping Louie (Buck) Newsom and others tiring, plus raw rookies, use some of that splendid baseball material that the town's fans saw. . . .

The splendid campaign of the trade union movement amongst the auto workers, which has resulted in hundreds of UAW baseball teams seeing Negro and white players this year jointly participating, must be carried over to the big leagues, and such material as Detroit fans saw on September 14, with the Monarchs and Chicago Giants, brought into big league baseball. Not being a reporter for baseball and sports activity (we leave that to the very capable Lester Rodney on our staff) in this piece we have done our best to "tell the story as we saw it."

But no coverage of the double-header between the Negro teams . . . would be complete unless we said something about the "coverage" of the local sewer sheets, the *Free Press,* the Hearst Press and the "liberal" *Detroit News.*

Like "sages" they condescended to "cover" the games. Sickening and nauseating are their saccharine discriminating "write-ups." Forced to write the games up because of 34,784 fans that left the ballpark wondering why Negro players are not in the big leagues, the "sages" of the press box proceed with their hatchets to depict Satchel Paige as one who "snoozed" along during the game. Last week the *Detroit News* ran a picture of Paige with the obvious filthy lie, stating that when the picture was taken the photographer asked Paige to smile and Paige is reported to have said, "Ah cain't smile, 'cause I just woked up."

To watch Paige pitch, to know the splendid athletes of the Negro people, is to take such a picture and rip it to shreds as a piece of vicious, anti-Negro propaganda emanating from "minds" like Ku Klux Klanners. To find that such a pitcher, such an athlete, is barred from big league baseball because he is a Negro makes one's blood boil and take the oath here and now that the campaign for Negro ball players to play in the big leagues is something you have neglected and must organize.

Oh, there is much more that one could say about these poison pen artists' barb-shooting against the fine Negro athletes playing all over the nation being barred from the big leagues. Detroit's trade union movement, that has written in letters of struggle that Negro and whites shall be united in unions, political action and social activity, must step up and take as healthy a cut at Jim Crowism as they have seen the Kansas City Monarchs and the Chicago Negro Giants take last Sunday. The ailing and ancient Tigers need such players, need such brilliant pitching and catching as we witnessed Sunday. Let's demand from Walter Briggs that Detroit shall have it and have it next season.

Reprinted from the Daily Worker, *September 15, 1941.*

Of the four Tiger teams to win world championships in the twentieth century, the 1945 Bengals have received the least acclaim, overwhelmed by the still-vivid memories of the 1968 and 1984 squads and lost in the warm, historic glow of the legendary 1935 champs, with their roster of four future Hall of Famers. But at the time the 1945 Tigers were widely celebrated, capping a momentous year that saw America victorious in World War II. Today, the series is more likely to be remembered as the one in which a Chicago bar owner cursed the Cubs for evicting his billy goat from the stands during game four. The Cubs have not since won a pennant.

1945

H. G. Salsinger

TNT

CHICAGO—They said they would win yesterday because they always won when they had to win and that is how it was.

They had half a dozen chances to win the sixth game on Monday and tossed them all off, enabling the Cubs to beat them in twelve innings, but that didn't affect them in the least.

"We've always won when we had to win, all season long, and we'll do it again this time. After all, this is just another series."

So it was to them, just another series, and they came through just as they had done all season long, in every crisis.

They didn't win the American League championship until the last day of the season, and they didn't win the World Series until the last game.

"You see, we do everything the hard way," explained Paul Richards.

When the final story of the American League season of 1945 is written, the main character will be Harold Newhouser.

It was Newhouser who pitched Detroit into first place in June, Newhouser who pitched them back into an undisputed lead when the New York Yankees tied them for first place, and Newhouser who got them back into the lead when the Yankees passed them.

It was Newhouser on whom Steve O'Neill relied in the seventh and deciding game of the World Series and his confidence was once more rewarded.

Detroit beat the Cubs with TNT, meaning Trucks, Newhouser and Trout, and they beat them twice with "N."

Newhouser had no luck in the first game of the series where Hank Borowy shut out the Tigers. In that game every break went against Newhouser and favored the Cubs.

He had little support in the fifth game, on Sunday, where he won by a score of 8-4 but where he deserved a shut out. As someone remarked later, he had to win a doubleheader beating both the Cubs and his own team.

The fortunes of baseball favored him yesterday. The Tigers scored five runs before Newhouser delivered his first pitch and with a five-run margin to work under he had a chance to finesse.

We do not recall ever seeing his curve break as well as it did yesterday. He had plenty of speed and a fine change of pace but it was his curveball that bewildered and befuddled the Cubs. They had not seen another quite like it before.

With all his stuff, Newhouser had grand control. He walked one batter and made one wild pitch but he struck out ten, including three pinch hitters.

Starting out under a five-run lead was a happy experience for Newhouser. Too many times this year was he forced to bear down all the way, hoping for a run or two.

He had a potent aide in Paul Richards, his battery mate, until a foul tip broke the little finger of his throwing hand in the eighth inning.

Richards came up with three on in his first inning and hit a base-clearing double. In the seventh he hit another double that drove in still another run so that Richards alone pounded in enough runs to make Newhouser the winning pitcher.

Chicago was favored to win the series because the Cubs were deeper in starting pitchers but they discovered that there is a difference between starting pitchers during the regular season and starting pitchers in the World Series.

Hank Wyse won twenty-two games during the season but he was of no help to the Cubs against Detroit.

Ray Prime won thirteen games before the World Series but all the luck he had against Detroit was bad. He had nothing to fool the Tigers.

Paul Derringer won sixteen games for the Cubs but he was a failure in three relief assignments.

With all his starting pitchers—and the Cubs had six of them during the season—Charlie Grimm was forced to use Hank Borowy four times.

Borowy shut out Detroit in the first game, was knocked out in the fifth game on Sunday, came in as relief pitcher in the ninth inning of the sixth game on Monday and won in twelve innings, and was back as starting pitcher yesterday.

Before the game Borowy said that he didn't think he would do much good. He can always come back the day after he pitches but is ineffective if he tries to come back after one day's rest. So he said and so it was.

Borowy pitched only seven balls in his last appearance and only three batters faced him. Each of them singled and he was charged with three runs in the Cubs' defeat. He became the first pitcher in World Series history to achieve a pitching record of two games won and two lost.

Six years ago Paul Derringer was famous as the best control pitcher in baseball. He still had the distinction when he beat Detroit in the seventh game of the 1940 World Series at Cincinnati. He was a master craftsman in those days.

The Derringer who relieved Borowy in the first inning yesterday with one run over, two runners on the bases and none out was a tenth carbon copy of the Derringer of 1940. Control was the one thing he had nothing of, as the boys say.

Greenberg, the first batter who faced Derringer, sacrificed [Roy] Cullenbine then received an intentional pass, filling bases. It seemed good strategy when [Rudy] York popped out. Derringer then walked [Jimmy] Outlaw on four pitches and forced in [Eddie] Mayo. He had Richards down one ball and two strikes when the Texan slashed his two-bagger into the left-field corner, driving home three runners.

After [James] Webb and Mayo flied out to start the second inning, Derringer got behind the next four batters. He was three-and-one with each of them. [Doc] Cramer singled and Greenberg, Cullenbine and York all walked, the York pass forcing in Cramer. That was the last of Derringer for 1945.

In one and one-third innings Derringer walked five batters and forced in two runs.

There was some very bad pitching in the series, also some very good pitching. It was on the whole a pitchers' series and demonstrated once more that in a seven-game engagement pitching is about eighty percent of the issue involved.

Hank Borowy in the first game. Virgil Trucks in the second. Claude Passeau's one-hit performance in the third. Paul Trout's historic achievement in the fourth. Harold Newhouser in the fifth and Newhouser again in the seventh. Only in the sixth game did neither side produce a dominant starting pitcher. In the other six games one pitcher was in full charge.

The Detroit pitching was better than Chicago's. The Cubs gave their pitchers much better outfield support. Detroit's out-fielding was the weakest ever seen in a World Series.

As usual most of the pre-series predictions were washed out in actual competition.

The Cubs were supposed to be helpless at Briggs Stadium but they won two out of three games played there.

The Tigers were presumably handicapped at Wrigley Field but they won three out of four games and the title there and should have had three straight.

The Cubs were expected to win because of pitching depth and superior strength at shortstop and in the outfield but the star shortstop of the series, and the star infielder for that matter, was James (Skeeter) Webb.

It was not a pleasant series for the home folks. The customers at Briggs Stadium and Wrigley Field had little to cheer about.

Detroit players last night said that the arrival of Virgil Trucks gave them the "shot in the arm" that they needed to win the title.

Trucks rejoined the club the day before the season closed. He started the final game against the St. Louis Browns but gave way to Newhouser in the sixth inning.

He pitched the second game of the World Series and beat the Cubs 4-1, tying the series at one-all. It was a vital game and had the Tigers failed to win it all, the World Championship pennant would be raised at Wrigley Field next summer instead of at Briggs Stadium.

For a three-year period, baseball had no better pitcher than Hal Newhouser. From 1944 to 1946, Newhouser averaged nearly twenty-seven victories a season, had an earned run average under two, and won a pair of Most Valuable Player awards. But his temperament wasn't always as pristine.

1947
Kyle Crichton

"PRINCE" HAL?

In past years Master Harold Newhouser, Detroit southpaw, was a nuisance of such unprecedented malignancy that only divine intervention saved him from lethal belaboring at the hands of his playmates. Now considered by many critics the greatest pitcher in baseball, there was a time when he not only failed to influence hitters but succeeded admirably in alienating friends.

"Let us observe merely that he is a thick-headed Dutchman," they used to say elegantly and bitterly in the Detroit dugout, stroking a bat tenderly and wishing the laws on assault were less stringent in Michigan.

This ordinarily followed a scene in which Master Hal welcomed a teammate's error by taking off his glove, putting his hands on his hips and glaring murderously at the offender. He would then return to the mound in a white rage and start throwing the ball toward the plate with insane fury. Since his brains and

Harold "Prince Hal" Newhouser

temper had left him simultaneously, there was nothing on the ball but anger, and the result was invariably disastrous. The harder Master Hal threw them up, the faster they came whistling back and it soon became a question not only of saving the game but of preserving Newhouser's life.

"I will not say that Newhouser was disliked," remarks a teammate who now finds him admirable, "but it is a happy chance that there is nobody on this club now serving time for homicide."

Newhouser gives credit for his reformation to his wife but this must be less than strictly accurate because the marriage was in 1941 and Hal was still playing Dracula in 1942 and 1943. The change came in 1944 when he won twenty-nine and lost nine and almost pitched Detroit into a pennant. For that chore he won the American League's most valuable player award and took it again in 1945, when he won twenty-five and lost the usual nine. Last year he won twenty-six and lost nine and compiled an earned-run average of 1.94. In 1945 it had been 1.81, the first time in twenty-seven years a pitcher had allowed an average of fewer than two runs a game two years in succession.

"The triumph of matter over mind," said some of his ill-wishers, but this is vigorously rebutted by the Detroit sports writers and most close followers of the game. "This young man will never rival Nietzsche as a thinker," says Harry Salsinger of the *Detroit News,* "but he will out pitch [Bob] Feller, [Spud] Chandler, [Boo] Ferriss or anybody in our league. I think he'll out pitch anybody in any league."

At twenty-six Newhouser is probably as immature as any man who ever dominated his profession. He is still a big blond kid and will possibly end that way. Rube Waddell would have had trouble matriculating at the Sorbonne and Dizzy Dean never conducted a seminar in his life, but they were large burly characters who make Newhouser look like someone who has wandered out of the Epworth League. It is only when he is on the mound that he grows into a magician. The gentry facing him would not thank us for hinting Hal is a child; they regard him simply as Attila, the Asiatic Scourge.

Newhouser's father ran a *Turnverein* (gymnasium) in Detroit and it was natural that Hal should be an athlete. His brother, Richard, four years older, was signed by Detroit and farmed out to Beckley and Charleston in the Middle Atlantic League and to Hot Springs in the Cotton States League but suffered a whack on the head from a pitched ball and gave up the silly profession. Hal first made the world sit up (the small world around Detroit) when he pitched for the Roose-Vanker Post of the American Legion in 1937, and struck out twenty-four batters of the Learned Post.

In his first year he won fourteen and lost two; in 1938 he won seventeen and lost one. In the latter year he allowed only four earned runs in eighteen games! When he lost to San Diego in the semifinals of the national legion championships at Charlotte, North Carolina, that year it was the first run scored off him in sixty-five innings. In that time he had pitched three no-hit games and run his string of victories to seventeen straight.

Then a happening occurred that may have been responsible for some of his later mishaps: Wish Egan, the Detroit scout, appeared at the Newhouser home to sign the boy. The family was rocking sedately on the front porch when the famous Wish turned up with five one-hundred-dollar bills and thrust four of them into Papa Newhouser's fist and one into the clammy paw of Harold.

Papa, who was only working three days a week at that time, gasped and said, "Isn't that a little high for a seventeen-year-old kid?" And Wish said no, sirree; that was just about the right figure and besides he had a contract here for a hundred and fifty a month and if Mr. Newhouser would just sign his name as father of this interesting minor, they could consider that a long and warm friendship had been launched.

Mr. Egan had no sooner departed with the document carefully wrapped within his bosom when a flashy convertible turned into the street and deposited Cy Slapnicka and Roger Peckinpaugh of the Cleveland Indians on the Newhouser front steps. There have been two versions of what happened next. One has it that Mr. Slapnicka tendered a bonus check of $15,000 and waved a hand at the convertible which was also to be part of the deal, while the Newhousers cradled their heads in their hands and cried oh-oh-oh! The other version is that Cy learned he was too late and then proffered the check and added, "The car is also yours!" Detroiters regard this as a typically Machiavellian trick by Slap to make young Newhouser dissatisfied with the Detroit deal.

Harold maintains now that he never gave the matter another thought but there is plain evidence that the Newhousers uttered at least a few anguished moans over the subject.

In any event Newhouser was sent down to the Detroit farm at Alexandria, Louisiana, where he won eight and lost four and was then dispatched posthaste to Beaumont in the Texas League. He won the first two and lost the next twelve, but looked so good that Detroit brought him up at the end of the season. He pitched one game against Cleveland and lost it.

Now began Childe Harold's battle against the fates. They had given him a great fastball, a good curve and a nice change of pace. But in a spirit of jolly fun they kept back one thing: victories. If Hal pitched a two-hitter, the other guy pitched a no-hitter. In the first twenty-one innings of the 1943 season Detroit got him only one run. Any time things got to looking too good for his cause, his teammates began playing a little game of their own called you-kick-this-one-I'll-kick-the-next. Soon Harold was talking to nobody but himself on the club.

He lost fourteen in 1942 and seventeen in 1943. This was the final straw and he went to Steve O'Neill, the new manager, and asked to be traded. "Traded, my eye," said Steve. "You're going to be one of my starting pitchers this year." Newhouser now gives O'Neill credit for straightening him out and utters most laudatory words about the Christian spirit Steve utilized in this venture, but the truth seems to be that Harold almost drove Steve mad before the turn came. At one point he came to O'Neill and said:

"Steve, you're riding me too hard."

"And I'm going to keep riding you," bellowed Steve, "till you stop being so damned dumb out there."

Newhouser lists four factors in his reformation: (a) his marriage, (b) the birth of his little girl in 1943, (c) O'Neill and (d) Paul Richards, the Detroit catcher. Although we have said his wife's influence was late in catching on, it is true that she has had a great deal to do with his success. She is widely admired around the Detroit club and Newhouser is literally wild about her and the baby. He is a boy with the finest instincts and much of his progress is due to his happy home life.

Paul Richards had been around a long time when he gave up the job of managing Atlanta to come back to Detroit, and the one thing he has learned in a busy life is never to give advice until it is asked for. Newhouser finally got around to asking Richards what he was doing wrong. They went out on the field.

"Listen," said Richards. "Try one outside, try one inside, one up here, one down here; throw the curve overhand, sidearm, natural. You can't do any worse, can you?"

Newhouser is now a pitcher with everything. He has three speeds for both his curve and fast one. Several years ago he picked up a slider. Birdie Tebbetts says the overhand curve is the best of all.

But even with his new stuff and confidence, Newhouser still had to get started right. There was always the feeling that the gods were going to cross him again. What changed him was a game in Cleveland.

"We're two runs behind and it doesn't look as if we're ever going to catch up," says Hal. "A young catcher named Hack Miller is up for us and there are two on. It's his first time at bat in the big leagues and what does he do? He hits the first ball for a home run against the railing in the big stadium. It bounces around out there till he gets over. That puts us ahead and that's the turning point for me. It's been good ever since."

The turnover in temperament didn't come all at once. Even then he couldn't stand to lose. He was losing in a game of hearts one night when he grabbed the cards, tore them up and slammed them around the hotel room.

"That's why I'm a great competitor," he yelled. "I hate to lose."

It is true that this is one of his great assets. He is in the class with Burleigh Grimes and Johnny Allen, who would cut your legs off at the knee if it won a ball game. And like other fighters, Newhouser is not afraid to throw it in when it counts.

"In the clutch," he says, "I give them my best pitches, the curve or the fast one. If it isn't enough, you know you've done your best anyhow. But if you used the slider and they conked it, you'd never stop kicking yourself."

If there has ever been any doubt about his courage (which there wasn't) it was dispelled in 1944, when he and Dizzy Trout were a team that pitched almost constantly. They were in forty-five of the last seventy-five games. The pair won thirty-three of the fifty-one victories in that stretch, saved two in relief and pitched two ties. They were in six of the last eight games. The St. Louis Browns won the pennant on the last day of the season but Newhouser won twenty-nine games and Trout twenty-seven for the season. As a two-punch pitching unit they broke all records for achievement. They won seven more than the famous Dizzy and Paul Dean combination in 1934; four more than Grove and Earnshaw in 1931 and one more than Stan Coveleski and Jim Bagby in 1920.

In 1945, Newhouser picked up a bad back in midseason and was in such pain that he was left behind when Detroit started on an Eastern trip. When the Tigers ran out of pitchers, Newhouser was flown from Detroit and pitched in the last game of the New York series. He got along all right until the Yanks filled the bases with Keller at bat. Until that time he hadn't thrown a curve; now he threw one and struck Keller out. It almost killed Hal and from then on he used nothing but his hard one and a change-up pitch. He beat them 4-0 and he considers it one of his greatest triumphs.

Newhouser is a peculiar individual in that he gains weight during the playing season and loses it in the winter. In his earlier days he lacked stamina ("seventh inning and then BAM!") and even now he needs eleven hours sleep a night. He can't eat after he pitches and never sleeps more than two or three hours a night after a game. Next day he can hardly walk from stiffness but he has a long sleep the second night and feels great the third day. He doesn't smoke and his attempts at drinking have been pitiful.

"I guess I just don't know how to do it," he says.

But for years he was one of the heaviest eaters in baseball. Dizzy Trout, who acts as the Newhouser Boswell, reports one occasion when the string bean won a bet with Dick Bartell by mangling fourteen steak sandwiches, three barbecued chicken sandwiches and two quarts of ice cream at a single sitting.

"How about a nice hunk of that roast beef?" suggested Trout.

"Shucks," said Hal modestly. "I don't want to make a hog of myself."

Newhouser says he never had a model as a pitcher and picked up his original style by monkeying with it. At the beginning of his career when he was eager to get all his strength into his pitches, he pulled his leg up so high his knee came between his hands on the windup. It was much like pitching out of a barrel and he has dropped that for the benefit of occasionally seeing his catcher. He had a knot in his shoulder for several years but seems to have grown out of it, just as he has the heart condition that kept him out of the service and for a time threatened to end his career. He has never had a sore arm in his life.

It can be said for him that he is not a prima donna when it comes to working. In 1944 and 1945 when the pennant was at stake he was in the bullpen steadily. He opened the present season in St. Louis on a day better fitted for arctic maneuvers than baseball. The game was halted once for thirty minutes and a second time for forty minutes by rain. This meant that Newhouser warmed up three times. He shut out the Browns, 7-0, with four hits. "Three games I pitched; that's all," he said proudly.

The Browns spent little time in admiration of the feat. With this game, Newhouser had beaten them thirteen times in a row and they were beginning to suspect that he had something they couldn't fathom.

It is possible to get in a fight in any bar or poolroom over the respective merits of Newhouser and Feller. Last year Bill Veeck rigged up a "Pitching Battle of the Century" or something in Cleveland between the two giants, and Newhouser blew Cleveland out of the park. He fanned nine, shut them out 4-0 and allowed only two men to reach first! Early this year the boys hitched up again and Feller had his fun. He beat Newhouser, 6-0, and allowed Detroit only three hits. So what does it all prove?

On the personal side, Newhouser is a strange contradiction. He is city-reared and yet he is as suspicious of strangers and as uncertain in life as any hillbilly. Once when a magazine writer wrote him for an interview and suggested that he was nuts not to take advantage of the opportunity, Newhouser considered that he was being called crazy and was greatly hurt. He now has an attorney friend in Detroit who handles his affairs and helps him with the Hal Newhouser fan clubs, which do good work in keeping youngsters occupied and out of trouble.

Perhaps some of his self-consciousness comes from a scar under his right eye, which was due to an infected pimple as a baby. If one catches him only from that side his face takes on an evil look, which is not warranted by his blond hair and pleasant ways.

According to accounts by Leo Macdonell of the *Detroit Times,* Hal is lucky to be alive. At the age of seven he fell off a woodpile onto a board full of spikes and punctured his stomach. At nine a playful companion opened his head with a brickbat; while playing basketball he got a floor burn which eventually turned into blood poisoning; in football he busted a few blood vessels.

Newhouser has the greatest respect for Vern Stephens, the St. Louis Browns' shortstop, considering him the best all-around player in the league. This is because Stephens pulverizes him when they meet. He has the usual trouble with Joe DiMaggio and Ted Williams but thinks Lou Boudreau of Cleveland is the smartest hitter of them all.

Joe Gordon has always given him trouble, but his headache for years was Bob Johnson, old left fielder for the Athletics and Red Sox. "He used to murder me," says Newhouser. "Batted .500 against me."

Newhouser is something of a Ring Lardner you-know-me-Al character with Boy Scout attachments. Like all players who have acquired the modern lore of the game, he finds Steve O'Neill the best manager in baseball, Mr. Briggs the finest owner in baseball and Detroit the greatest town to play in. He says he has never dickered over salary or held out for a better contract, but the Detroit writers lift a questioning brow at this.

In any event, Detroit has treated him well and he has treated Detroit well. He is said to have been paid $45,000 in 1946 and to have signed for $50,000 this year. In addition there have been bonuses.

"He's not the gentlest character out there," says [Birdie] Tebbetts, who used to catch for him, "but he wants to win. I know a lot of pleasant guys who never win."

Copyright 1947, Collier's.

Harry Heilmann may be the most underappreciated Tiger. Though his career aver-age of .342 is second only to Ty Cobb's among Detroiters, he failed to make the all-time Tiger team when fans last voted in 1999. He died in 1951 before being inducted into the Baseball Hall of Fame, prompting national tributes like this one in the New York World-Telegram and Sun.

1951

Dan Daniel

TOO LATE

DETROIT—Harry Edwin Heilmann, one of the greatest right-handed batters baseball yet has boasted, a gentleman of exemplary repute on and off the field, and for many years militant for the game as a broad-caster, died here yesterday, at the age of 56, of cancer of the lung.

Heilmann, who should have been elected to the Hall of Fame years ago, died without having achieved the diamond pantheon at Coopers-town, NY.

Both the baseball writers, who vote on candidates who have ended their playing careers not more than twenty-five years ago, and the Hall of Fame Committee, which passes on the merits of old-timers, appear to be obsessed with the fear lest some of the diamond's titans slip past their cordon while yet alive.

As a consequence, Heilmann passed on to baseball's Valhalla minus an honor which he and his family would have appreciated so tremendously.

Some weeks ago, the doctors at Ford Hospital told Harry Salsinger, sports editor of the *Detroit News,* that Heilmann would not survive the summer.

Harry Heilmann's Hall of Fame plaque

Salsinger, Joe Williams and the writer then organized a movement to have Harry named to the Hall of Fame. A scroll of official notification was to be presented to him or Mrs. Heilmann at home plate just before today's All-Star game.

The mills of the Hall of Fame Committee grind slowly. Ever so slowly. Although a precedent had been set, in a similar situation, in the election of the tragic Lou Gehrig, the committee refused to take it upon itself to designate Heilmann, who was far more entitled to the honor than some of the old-timers who had been chosen by that group.

It was decided to have a midsummer election by the baseball writers, and if Heilmann could achieve the minimum of 75 percent of the total vote cast, he would be an official, bona-fide, honest-to-goodness member of the Hall of Fame.

Ty Cobb heard about the movement to have Heilmann elected, and never stopped to consider the possibility that the Hall of Fame Committee would refuse to make an exception. . . .

Cobb wrote to Harry and told him he was about to be named to baseball's galley of immortals. Ty unwittingly performed a benefice.

In any event, poor Harry could not wait for the projected mid-summer poll. He could not wait for the hidebound committee to recede one iota from its rules and regulations.

In effect the committee said, "If Harry should pass away before we can do anything about electing him, it will be too bad. We earnestly advise Heilmann to hang on until we can get our machinery in motion.

"Election to the Hall of Fame is very serious business, and we must not allow ourselves to be stampeded by anything so inconsequential as medical prediction that the candidate cannot survive much longer."

The committee in all its rectitude might have rushed a call through the press association wires for all eligible voters of the Baseball Writers Association of America to mail their ballots to Ken Smith, secretary of that organization, in time to determine whether Heilmann could be honored at home plate today.

But no action was taken. And now Harry is gone, and the need for an emergency election is gone with him.

The Hall of Fame Committee is composed of Connie Mack, Edward G. Barrow, Bob Quinn, Del Webb, Grantland Rice and Paul Kerr, secretary.

It would be interesting to know how many of these men were involved in the decision which refused Heilmann his supreme baseball citation while he yet was alive, fighting a cancer which was even more malignant than the doctors knew.

Heilmann's designation certainly would have entailed no deviation from the Hall of Fame slogan, "It's got to be tough to get in."

Harry won the American League batting championship no fewer than four times—.394 in 1921, .403 in 1923, .393 in 1925 and .398 in 1927. Heilmann's career average, covering eighteen years, was .342. Only six boast lifetime records superior to his.

Cobb tops the list with .367, then come [Rogers] Hornsby, .358; Dan Brouthers, .348; Ed Delehanty, .346; Willie Keeler, .345; and Tris Speaker, .344. Babe Ruth hit .342 and so did Jess Burkett. George Sisler as well as Gehrig made the .340 level.

The fact is that the Hall of Fame system needs overhauling, from top to bottom. The chief fault, I am sorry to say, rests with the baseball writers. Several years ago I participated in counting the ballots in an election. And some of the players who were honored with votes could not have carried Heilmann's shoes.

More Tiger fans remember George Kell as an announcer than as a player. But in the late 1940s and early 1950s Kell reigned as the American League's best third baseman and Detroit's top hitter. He edged Ted Williams for the batting title in 1949.

1952

William Barry Furlong

THE UNLIKELY HITTER

"He'll never be a ballplayer," said Larry MacPhail. "You'll never be a hitter," Al Simmons and Connie Mack told him. So George Kell, a man with natural disadvantages, beat Ted Williams in batting—and became the first big-leaguer to throw a man out while unconscious.

Baseball is essentially a business of muscles, with success riding on sharpness of reflexes and wholeheartedness of effort. Only occasionally, in this swing-from-the-heels era, does a ballplayer rise above the rest by using his head. One such man is George Kell of the Detroit Tigers, who is generally regarded as the best third baseman in the game.

A self-made batsman in the old scientific tradition of hit-'em-where-they-ain't, he is always a good bet to finish among the five leading hitters in the American League. As a fielder, he has the variables of his position so exhaus-

tively analyzed that he has a boundless capacity for making the spectacular look routine. His ball club was way off the pace all last year, but Kell stayed near the top of the player heap.

Being the undemonstrative, no-fanfare type, both in and out of uniform, George Kell is not the kind of ballplayer who lends himself to catchy sports-page tag lines. The late Harry Heilmann, who himself won four American League batting titles with the Tigers and more recently functioned as a Detroit baseball broadcaster, came as close as anyone to pin-pointing what makes Kell a standout.

"George is the quarterback of the team," Heilmann said not long before his death last July. "George is all brains out there."

Every major-league hitter worthy of the name tries to adapt himself to the various opposing pitchers, but few carry things as far as George Kell. For example, whereas the average hitter always takes up the same stance, Kell is constantly maneuvering for advantage in the batter's box. If he's facing a fastball hurler, he stands far in the rear of the box to get as long a look at the pitch as possible before he has to swing. Against a curve-ball specialist, he moves closer to the front of the box to get the wood on the ball before it has much chance to break.

"Sometimes I'll shift two or three times on a single pitcher, just to keep him off balance," Kell declares. Lyall Smith, sports editor of the *Detroit Free Press*, reports that he has seen Kell take up as many as four different positions in a single turn at bat.

On defense, Kell has been blessed with a strong, accurate arm and a pair of deft, steady hands. "If he gets his hands on a ball," says manager Red Rolfe of the Tigers, "he holds onto it." Once again, however, it is mental application that has made Kell not merely a good fielding third baseman but a great one. He catalogues the batting and running potentialities of each hitter and plays them accordingly. As a result, he invariably seems to be in the right spot at the right time.

The toughest hitters for a third baseman to play are those who are capable both of beating out bunts and of pulling the ball hard down the third-base line, like Phil Rizzuto of the Yankees and Orestes Minoso and Chico Carrasquel of the White Sox. Kell says that you have to risk the hard shots and play in a little on these fellows. "If you play back, they're sure to bunt and get a hit," he declares.

Kell studies the condition of the infield before every game. Not only does he check on whether it's smooth or lumpy, soft or hard, but he also examines the texture of the dirt. "If the dirt is tight," he explains, "the ball will take a better bounce. If it's loose, you have to be prepared for anything."

Like an earlier Detroit infield star, silent Charlie Gehringer, George Kell has won recognition on sheer merit rather than showmanship. If Kell is anything other than a mild-mannered, even-tempered, thoroughly pleasant young man, there is no evidence to indicate it. However, although he has his emotions under control, he is not stolid or phlegmatic. On the field he frequently seems to be wearing a slight frown. "I've noticed it around the house, too," says his father. "He looks like he just sinks into a deep study." Kell is a bear-down ballplayer—all the great ones are. He throws himself with utter absorption into every game. Some people will tell you that under the surface he is still as tightly wound as the greenest rookie before the start of each contest.

None of his internal tension seems to erupt on the ball field. As far as anyone can remember, the nearest he ever came to losing his temper was after pitchers had sent him sprawling into the dirt some fifteen times during May and June of 1949. Even then, about all he said was, "Something ought to be done about pitchers throwing at a batter. Somebody is going to get hurt someday."

Off the field, Kell makes himself even less conspicuous. He is not given to late hours or drinking. He's a homebody who dislikes road trips because they take him away from his wife and two youngsters. He was born, raised and still makes his off-season home in the small town of Swifton, Arkansas—population 526. He never would have thought of leaving home if it hadn't been for baseball. In short, George Kell is the classic rebuttal to the viewpoint that "nice guys finish last."

But brains are Kell's most distinctive attribute. He is not notably well equipped physically for playing baseball. Although he's inclined to be stocky—he plays at 180 pounds and stands only five feet nine inches tall—he is not a power hitter. Not only does his running have a hint of the hunched, labored intensity of a well-upholstered catcher, but he has been burdened since birth with loose cartilage in both knees, a condition which caused him to be rejected for military service in World War II. The knees don't pop out of joint; they simply swell up and ache intensely whenever he plays for a long stretch without rest.

Kell's shrewdness is not manifest in his features, which radiate good-natured innocence. Of German-Irish ancestry, he has a sturdy jaw, wavy, red-tinged hair and dancing blue eyes. He dresses elegantly but conservatively. Except for a tendency to indulge in the colloquialisms of his native Arkansas—he might say, for instance, "That happened about six mile up the road"—his carefully precise grammar reflects both his education and upbringing.

Kell's complete concentration on the game was most memorably demonstrated on August 29, 1948. The Tigers were struggling to protect a 2-1 lead over the New York Yankees in Yankee Stadium. In the sixth inning the Yankees loaded the bases and Joe DiMaggio came to bat. DiMag slashed a vicious grounder down the third-base line that took an erratic hop just in front of Kell.

"I can remember seeing the ball take the hop and turning my head," says George. The ball crunched against Kell's right jaw, breaking it in two places, just below the ear and just above the chin. Although he blacked out—he can't remember anything that happened on the field after he turned his head—Kell scooped up the ball and got over to third for a force-out. Then he began lurching around the diamond like a drunk groping for the bar.

When his head finally cleared, after they had led him away and put him under a shower, the first words he mumbled were, "Did I get the man out?"

As a rule, Kell uses his head for something besides stopping ground-balls. Despite his obvious lack of speed, he's led the American League third basemen in the fielding averages four times: in 1945, 1946, 1950, and 1951. His handsome fielding statistics haven't been due to an inability to reach balls other third basemen could handle; in three of four years he led the third basemen in fielding he also led them in chances accepted.

In addition to his mental index on where each batter is likely to hit, Kell has a remarkable knack for getting the jump on the ball. As the pitcher reaches the climax of his windup, Kell takes one stride forward on his left foot and dips into a low, springy crouch. Whether the ball is hit right at him or to the side, whether it's hit sharply or slowly, Kell gets that fraction-of-a-second start that can mean the difference between a base hit and an out.

When he came up to the American League with the Philadelphia Athletics in 1944 and 1945, Kell was considered valuable chiefly because of his fielding. In those two years, he batted only .268 and .272. Says Kell now, "Everybody—even Connie Mack and Al Simmons—kept telling me, 'George, you'll be a great fielder, but you'll never be a hitter.'"

Kell refused to accept this verdict. He set about inflating his batting average as methodically as a research scientist isolating a new element. Severely self-analytical, George recognized that he wasn't a power hitter. In four years in the minor leagues he hit only six home runs; in his first eight years in the majors, he was to add only twenty-eight. Consequently, he tailored his batting technique to fit his particular strength—place hitting. He selected a bat that measures thirty-four inches and weighs but thirty-two ounces, one of the lightest in the American League. Although a right-handed batter, he had been hitting almost exclusively to right and right-center fields. Now he spread his hands on the bat and learned to pull to left, until he could spray hits to all fields with equal skill.

Studying other batters—especially place hitters like Luke Appling, the former shortstop of the Chicago White Sox—he discovered that there is no single batting technique. "Everybody should bat the way that's best for him as an individual," he says. Kell evolved a style all his own, manipulating the bat in various ways for precision marksmanship, and, as previously related, shifting around to different points of vantage in the batter's box.

The success of Kell's scientific approach to batting is mirrored in the averages. In 1946, his first season with the Tigers, he spurted to .322— exactly fifty points higher than his 1945 mark. He hit .320 in 1947 and .304 in 1948—a year when he missed more than one third of the season because of injuries. Since then he's always been well above the .300 level.

"George has a base-hit swing," says Jerry Priddy, second baseman of the Tigers. "You can't gang up on him to cut off hits," says former teammate Saul Rogovin, now pitching for the White Sox, "because he can hit any pitch anyplace he wants." Art Houtteman, the young Tiger pitching star who was discharged from the Army last fall, used to declare admiringly, "One way or another, he's going to get that good batting average every year. There's no question about it. He's going to do it!"

Characteristically, Kell minimized the effect of his studies. "When I came up to the Athletics in 1944, I was just a kid of twenty-one making the jump from Class B ball," he says. "Those first two years in the major leagues were years I might have spent in the minors if it hadn't been for the war. So, when I began hitting in 1946, I really was just ready for major-league pitching."

Around the American League, Kell has been labeled a first-ball hitter and a bad-ball hitter. Both beliefs, neither precisely accurate, stem from the same tactic: Kell's determination not to get behind the pitcher on the count. Many players make a policy of allowing the first pitch to go by without offering more than an incurious glance. In effect, Kell reasons, that cuts the number of strikes allowed the batter to two, since the pitcher inevitably will put the first pitch in the strike zone if he knows the batter won't swing at it. Consequently, Kell is always ready to swing at the first pitch, although he'll refuse to bite if it isn't to his liking.

Whatever the count, he frequently swings at pitches that aren't in the strike zone. "If a pitch is anywhere near the plate and it's one you like, you might as well swing at it because you might not see it again," he says. But Kell seldom goes for any really bad pitch. He struck out only eighteen times in 598 times at bat last year, while he drew sixty-one walks.

George Clyde Kell was born on August 23, 1922, the oldest of three sons to Alma and Melvin Clyde Kell. One brother, Frank, a fire lieutenant in the Air Force, died in December 1946 in Frankfurt, Germany, the victim of a faulty gas heater. Another brother, twenty-two-year-old Everett—known best as "Skeeter"—batted .353 for Cordele, Georgia, in the Georgia-Florida League in 1950. A second baseman, Skeeter moved up to Savannah, Georgia, in the Class A South Atlantic League last year and came up to the Philadelphia Athletics for a spring-training trial this year.

As a youngster, George absorbed the lore and strategy of baseball from his father. A spirited, young-looking man of fifty-two, the elder Kell gave up playing semipro baseball only three and one-half years ago. Raised on a farm about twenty-five miles north of Swifton, Clyde Kell was the most coveted pitcher in Northeast Arkansas thirty years ago. In 1921, just before he married a pretty colleen named Alma Lorraine Perrin, Clyde Kell received a delegation of citizens from Swifton.

"Clyde," said one, "we've got a pretty good team down in Swifton, but we need another pitcher. Now, if you could see your way clear to come down and pitch for us, we'd be glad to set you up in business with a barbershop."

"Well, now," Clyde Kell replied. "That's all right with me—as long as it's all right with Alma, too." No less a baseball fan than her husband-to-be, Alma readily agreed. For twenty-two years, until he gave up barbering to open an electrical-appliance shop in 1943, Clyde Kell was Swifton's only barber. A wily hurler, with as many tricks as he had pitches, he pitched two or three times a week, winning at least seventy-five percent of his starts during his peak years between 1921 and 1931.

After every local baseball game, the Swifton semipro nine trooped over to Kell's barbershop for a shave and a shower. (Kell had the only public shower in town.) Young George listened in fascination to the bull sessions about the games. As he grew older, he spent more and more time applying his lessons on the diamond, and less and less time applying his energies to picking cotton in the local cotton fields for fifty cents a day.

"I told the boys to forget about working and to play all the baseball they wanted," says George's father. "I couldn't get enough of it when I was a boy, what with working all week on the farm and then walking five miles on Saturday afternoon to pitch a game."

George says he was never anything but an average student in school, but Lonnie Etheridge, who was superintendent and basketball coach at Swifton High School, remembers George as outstanding both scholastically and athletically.

"I knew him better as a basketball player than as a baseball player," says Etheridge. "He was one of those very rare boys—about one in every two hundred that come along, I guess—who had the ability to grasp a situation and find a solution almost immediately. I could explain a play to the team and in ten minutes George knew the exact movements of every player. I used to keep him on the bench beside me during the first few minutes of every game. We'd talk over the strategy being used by the other team and how we could overcome it. Then I'd send George in and he'd take complete control of the game. I think we won about twenty-seven out of thirty games that way when George was a junior—and you have to remember that he was no more than five feet five inches tall then and weighed only about 125 pounds."

Etheridge's influence extended far beyond the basketball court. A sincere, quietly religious man, he provided the intelligent away-from-home guidance that can be so essential to high-school youngsters. To this day George has never smoked—he appears in cigarette ads, but with the stipulation that he never be pictured smoking. He seldom drinks so much as a glass of beer.

Before he turned fifteen, George was playing with the American Legion club in Newport, Arkansas, then a town of about 4300, some twenty miles south of Swifton on U.S. Route 67. Shortly after George graduated from high school, Fred (Crackie) Parker, business manager of the now defunct Newport club in the equally defunct Newport Arkansas League, approached him. "Whenever you're ready to play professional ball, George," he said, "just let me know."

George went to Arkansas State College at Jonesboro for a year. In

June of 1940 he hunted out Parker. "I'm ready now, Crackie," he said, and promptly signed a contract for sixty dollars a month. Kell's debut in organized baseball was memorable if not encouraging. Playing short-stop, he scooped up a ground ball and made a monumental heave over the catcher's head, which allowed the tying and winning runs to score. In forty-eight games with Newport in 1940, he batted an exceedingly mod-est .160.

Scouts from the Brooklyn Dodgers were singularly unimpressed by the little infielder. Andy High, who supervised Brooklyn's scouting oper-ations in that area, apparently tried to soften up George for the eventual blow. "George," he said, "you'll never be a big-leaguer until you know the disappointment of being released by some club."

Instead of returning to college, George worked at various jobs around Swifton, picking up some extra change and courting pretty, blond Charlene Felts, whom he had met first in the sixth grade at Swifton Grammar School. On March 24, 1941, they were secretly mar-ried. They didn't break the news to their parents for more than three months. Now they have two youngsters, George, Jr., who is six, and Ter-rye Jane, who is two.

In 1941 George batted .310—almost double his figure in 1940—and sparked Newport to the pennant in both halves of a split season. At the close of the campaign, the Dodgers ordered him to report to their minor-league training base at Durham, North Carolina, the next spring.

When he reported to Durham, Kell was as streamlined and graceful as a wheelbarrow. Not only were his knees giving him unusual trouble but he was a flabby fifteen pounds overweight. One afternoon Larry MacPhail, then general factotum of the Dodgers, saw Kell floundering around third base.

"What's he doing here?" he demanded in a low scream. Fresco Thompson, then a bird dog in the Brooklyn scouting organization and now a vice-president of the Dodgers, tried to explain that George was an infielder who had hit .310 in a Class D league where the averages weren't very high.

"Well, get rid of him," snapped MacPhail. "He'll never be a ballplayer." Just thirteen days after he reported to Durham, George was handed his release. Andy High's prophecy was on its way to fulfillment— to the eventual regret of the Dodgers.

Even before he was cast adrift, Kell had been tempted to abandon the game. He listened with fascination when a construction foreman who roomed in the same boarding house described the lavish riches that were to be had by working on the Fort Bragg project. To Kell, who was then drawing $125 a month, the starting wage of $360 a month sounded sinful in its extravagance. At the invitation of the foreman, he journeyed out to Fort Bragg to size up the situation. "It looked like a good deal to me, so I called up my wife to talk to her about taking the job. She had a fit," he confesses with a sheepish grin, "so I stayed in baseball."

On the day that Kell was released by the Dodgers, the Lancaster, Pennsylvania, club of the Class B Inter-State League, a farm club of the Athletics, was in Durham for an exhibition game. George went over to see Tom Oliver, then manager of Lancaster and now a coach of the Athletics. "Do you need an extra infielder?" he asked.

"Can you play second base?" countered Oliver. George had never played the position.

"Sure," he said.

"You're on," said Oliver. Kell started the 1942 season at second base, shifted to first when the regular first baseman was injured, and eventually played shortstop and the outfield before settling down to third base. He batted .299 for the season.

"George had only one really serious fault when he joined us," says Oliver. "He had a tendency to back up on the ball instead of charging it. I'll say this for him: He'd wear you out correcting his weaknesses. He never made the same mistake twice while he was playing for me." Charging the ball is, of course, one of Kell's strongest points today.

Kell topped all the hitters of organized baseball in 1943 with a batting average of .396 and led Lancaster to the pennant and victory in the playoffs. He hit only five home runs all year, but one of them came on the night Connie Mack journeyed over from Philadelphia to scout the rotund third baseman personally. Kell joined the Athletics for a week at the end of the 1943 campaign, moving up permanently in 1944.

While his hitting was somewhat short of phenomenal during those first two years at Philadelphia, Kell's smartness and all-round competence made him a valuable prospect. A number of clubs sought him, including the Tigers, who were searching for a replacement for the aging Pinky Higgins. Then, in the middle of May in 1946, Connie Mack made his maiden trip on the newly installed elevator at Briggs Stadium and walked into the office of General Manager George Trautman, now president of the National Association of Minor Leagues.

"How would you like to have a third baseman?" asked Mr. Mack.

"What do you mean?" responded Trautman as warily as a man evading a subpoena server.

"I mean that I've got a third baseman you want and you've got an outfielder—Barney McCosky—that I want," said Mr. Mack. Trautman shuddered and described in dramatic detail the evils that would befall him should he part with McCosky, a highly popular product of Detroit's sandlots who had batted .316 in four pre-service years with the Tigers.

"Well, think it over," said Mr. Mack. Actually Trautman didn't have to think it over. The Tigers were as desperate for a third baseman as they were surfeited with outfielders. The following day, May 18, 1946, Kell and McCosky swapped uniforms.

Kell has never given Detroit fandom an opportunity to brood over the deal. His value to the Tigers extends far beyond the .327 batting average he has assembled in six years at Detroit. "Not only is George smart but he's aggressive," says Red Rolfe. "I don't mean he picks fights. I mean that he's always on the alert, looking for the breaks and helping to make them happen. And above all, he has baseball savvy."

Not until he edged out Ted Williams for the American League batting title in 1949 did Kell achieve real fame. In one of the closest batting races in American League history, Kell and Williams scrambled for the lead all year. Ted entered the final week of the season with a five-point bulge on George. That lead melted like fat in a frying pan until the final day, when George lashed out two hits in three trips to the plate off Bob Lemon of Cleveland, for whom he has a deep respect.

Meanwhile, Williams collected only one hit in his last eleven trips to the plate as Boston lost the pennant to the New York Yankees on the final day of the season. So by a margin of .0002 of a point—.3429 to .3427—Kell prevented Williams from becoming the first batter since Ty Cobb to win the American League batting crown three times in a row and a total of five times.

Curiously, Kell's triumph was received in many precincts with displeasure. A lot of people regarded the Tiger third baseman as an impertinent usurper, a "cheese champion" who couldn't repeat. Kell didn't quite repeat in 1950, but he did bat .340 in 157 games, finishing second to Billy Goodman, Boston's versatile handyman, who batted .354 in only 110 games.

Kell led both major leagues in hits—218—and doubles—fifty-six. He spanked 101 runs across the plate, the highest number in his career. Kell himself believes that he enjoyed his best season in 1950, a conviction he expressed so eloquently that the Tigers boosted his salary to an estimated $40,000. In 1951 he was among the first five hitters again with .319, topped only by Ferris Fain of the Athletics and Minnie Minoso of the White Sox, and he once more led his league in total hits.

Kell has been named to the last five American League All-Star teams. He missed the 1948 game because of injuries. In 1950 he got the highest total of any major-league player in the fan balloting, with 1,132,954 votes, compared to 1,061,522 for Jackie Robinson of the Dodgers and 1,041,396 for Williams. In a poll conducted by the Associated Press last spring among American League ballplayers, Kell was the only unanimous choice for All-Star laurels.

Although hardly the skylarking, hail-fellow type, Kell is not only respected but popular with his colleagues. He is one of those improbable characters for whom nobody seems to have a bad word. He rooms with Charley Keller on Tiger road trips. He does quite a bit of bridge playing with Keller, Freddy Hutchinson and Hoot Evers.

Naturally Kell enjoys a tremendous personal popularity with manager Red Rolfe. As a former ace third baseman, Rolfe can appreciate Kell's adroitness in the field. As a manager, Rolfe can appreciate Kell's artistry at bat. But most of all, he can appreciate the fact that Kell is the type of player who doesn't have to be "managed." George has the perception to recognize all alternatives in a given situation and the intelligence to pick the proper one.

When the season ends, not even attractive off-season propositions can keep him in Detroit. "One firm offered him as much as $15,000 to work for them during the winter," says his father. But George went back as usual to his neat, unpretentious eight-room home in Swifton. During the war he taught history and physical education in Swifton High School while Charlene taught third grade in Swifton Grammar School. He relaxes by going duck hunting with Lonnie Etheridge and by working his 520-acre farm about six miles north of Swifton.

Now twenty-nine, Kell considers his farm good insurance against the future. Even the modest returns of the first three years haven't dimmed his delight with the place. He gets up every morning and hustles out to the farm with the eagerness of a youngster bolting for the fireplace on Christmas morning. He has about half of the 520 acres out to pasture and sown with feed crops: barley, wheat and soybeans. He has stocked it with about sixty head of Angus cattle and seventy hogs. He'd like to expand his holdings to as much as 1500 acres.

Kell may never have the opportunity to retire to the farm. "He's big-league managerial timber," says one veteran baseball observer. "He's smart, he knows the game and he's got the knack of making the boys work with him."

Meanwhile, despite his brilliant present and his bright future, Kell is neither smug nor complacent. "There's still a lot to learn," he says. "You watch the different hitters—they don't have to be great batters—and you learn something new every day. You try it out. If it works, fine. If it doesn't, you try something else. But you never stop watching and you never stop learning."

Reprinted with permission of the Saturday Evening Post, *copyright 1952 (renewed), BFL&MS, Inc., Indianapolis.*

Days before the start of the 1960 season, Detroit and Cleveland shocked fans by swapping star players. The Tigers sent the defending American League batting champion, Harvey Kuenn, to the Indians for the holder of the home-run crown, Rocky Colavito. It was a controversial trade, for each man was well liked by the hometown fans. In his first at-bat as a Tiger at Briggs Stadium, Colavito helped mute the criticism by slugging a home run.

1960

Doc Greene

HARVEY FOR ROCKY

Harvey Kuenn is probably a better baseball player than Rocco Domenico Colavito ever will be. This is an opinion and not a fact which is an explanative courtesy that should be accorded the reader.

However, this was an excellent trade that [Tigers president] William DeWitt from St. Louis consummated with Frank Lane in Memphis yesterday and then informed Rick Ferrell and Jim Dykes in Lakeland so the bit might be announced.

It was excellent for several reasons.

In the first place, the various citizens who had wandered in and out of the Detroit Tiger front office during the recent search for management have always threatened to trade a real live ball player. No one was safe. No one was sacrosanct. But trades always involved an exchange of broken bats, used baseballs and a general reshuffling of mediocre names.

As Kuenn said last night, "I was shocked a little, but I

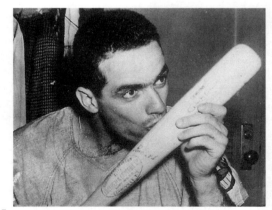

Rocky Colavito

hadn't worried about being traded. If I worried about these rumors, I couldn't do anything else. Every year I was going to be traded to someone."

But DeWitt traded an untouchable.

He could have done it more safely if he were concerned about public opinion. He could have waited until after the season had begun. If the Tigers got off well, he could have done nothing and worn a mantle of wisdom. But he made an eleventh hour deal, which must fall into the interests of forthrightness if nothing else.

If the trade between Cleveland and Detroit turns into a fiasco for the people who daily pay to imprison themselves at Briggs Stadium on summer afternoons, it was still excellent. You get a notion that someone is trying, a notion that has been absent.

But by now a man might be wondering about the statement concerning the relative talents of these two folk who live by the bat, ball and glove.

Statistics will show that Rocky Colavito shared the home run kingdom last season with Harmon Killebrew, of the last-place Washington Senators, at forty-two.

It will show that Kuenn, as American League batting champion, outhit his replacement by nearly a hundred points, .353 to .257. Rocky drove in 111 runs and Harvey managed seventy-one. Kuenn hit nine home runs. Kuenn also scored ninety-nine runs to Rocky's ninety. He stole seven bases and Rocky stole three.

Let the statisticians fish their conclusions from this.

The statement as to these two people's relative worth also includes the intangibles that abound in any business—and is there any doubt that this is one of those as well as being what is euphemistically called a sport?

Harvey was player representative for the Tigers and there is one from each club. When the eight got together, he was elected representative for the league. In other words, Kuenn speaks to American League management for the players.

This indicates respect. What, asks the man with monocle, has that got to do with the mechanics of winning ball games? Well, this, mister: Kuenn has an influence on his fellow man in knickers. Rocky is a delightful man of twenty-six, three years Harvey's junior. Rocky will influence no one. He's just a guy you like. In a slump, like the dandy he had late last summer when it must have occurred to Frank Lane to seek a trade, Rocky will not help. Kuenn sometimes did.

Colavito is not faster than Harvey. If he is, he doesn't apply it as well. In the outfield Colavito has a stronger arm although he probably may not cover the same ground. A third base coach once remarked, "I like to send runners in on Colavito because he might throw the ball into the upper deck. On the other hand, if he's on target, he'll throw my runner out. He's got a great arm, but it's scattery and then he might not throw to the right base."

Kuenn looks awkward, but gets the ground covered and instinctively throws to right bases all the time.

But it was a fine trade because of the stand DeWitt took and you can't give it that "same old Tigers" cynicism with Colavito around.

And he might hit all kinds of home runs in the Detroit park. It's generally shorter to left field for a right-hander here. And whether he does or not, a fan, even one who doted on Harvey, will like him. An interesting statistic, though, is that he hit one here a year ago, three last year for a total of four.

This feature provides a glimpse of two Detroit legends relatively early in their careers—popular first baseman Norm Cash and sportswriter Joe Falls. Cash, a fan favorite, played fifteen years with the Bengals, none more statistically amazing than his second in Detroit, when he led the league with a .361 average. Falls wrote about the Tigers for a half century, inspiring a generation of young sports journalists and earning a spot among the writers inducted in the National Baseball Hall of Fame.

1962

Joe Falls

STORMIN' NORMAN

Of all the names that made big headlines in baseball last year, none was more unexpected than that of Norm Cash. There was no ballplayer whose heroics embarrassed more people, either.

When the twenty-six-year-old country boy from Texas suddenly vaulted from the rank and file to the star class, he painfully surprised such seasoned baseball executives as Bill Veeck and Frank Lane, each of whom once held title to him but blithely traded him away. Cash even caught the home baseball public in Detroit off guard, although he had been with the Tigers throughout the previous year.

Take Mrs. Carl Williams, who lives down the street from Billy Hoeft, a former Tiger pitcher now with the Baltimore Orioles. When she heard that Norm Cash and his wife Myrta had rented the Hoeft house for the 1961 season, she smiled innocently and said, "That's nice. Is he a pitcher, too?"

It wasn't long before Mrs. Williams and every other Detroiter with the slightest interest in the Tigers was aware that Norman Dalton Cash was not a pitcher but a devastating left-hand-hitting first baseman in the tradition of the late Lou Gehrig. Cash always did resemble Gehrig a little, with his

brawny arms, piano legs and ready smile. Last year he began hitting like Gehrig, with a high average plus power. He did much to change Detroit from a sixth-place club into a pennant contender.

In the batting percentages Cash led the regulars of both major leagues with .361. He finished so far ahead of his closest American League competitor—teammate Al Kaline, who batted .324—that there was no real drama or suspense. For a while Yankee catcher Elston Howard, who ended up at .348, was pressing him. Howard didn't play every day, though, and by the middle of the season it became clear that he wouldn't have enough plate appearances to qualify for the batting title in any event.

Cash did not threaten Babe Ruth's home-run record. However, he not only out-hit Roger Maris by ninety-two points and Mickey Mantle by forty-four but also delivered plenty of long balls. He ranked fourth in the league in runs batted in with 132 and sixth in home runs with forty-one.

Norm Cash doesn't try for homers but he hits them anyway. He has a quick, compact swing that generates surprising power. He feels he helped himself by switching in 1960 from a thirty-three-ounce bat to the lightweight model of thirty-one ounces that is so popular among the modern sluggers.

There is no mistaking Cash for a bookkeeper or a banker or even a sports writer. He is a baseball player and he acts like one. He has such standard hobbies as hunting, fishing and golf. On the road he kills time by going to the movies, watching television or just lounging around and talking with his quiet, folksy roommate Frank Lary.

A solidly built six-footer of 190 pounds, he bounces when he walks. It is almost a swagger and gives him an air of self-confidence, which he happens to possess in abundance.

Some of the rival Yankees have gone so far as to term him "cocky"—a strong rap in the trade. However, if this were really true, Norm would not be the well-liked individual that he is in his own clubhouse.

He has great natural ability, of course, and this impresses ballplayers more than anything else. But beyond that, his Tiger teammates like Cash because he is a friendly fellow who takes his work seriously but not himself.

Fair-skinned and boyish-looking, he kids about his appearance. His lips frequently crack and blister from the sun, and glancing in the mirror Cash will say something like, "And now we would like you to meet Norm Cash, the new president of the Ugly Club."

After he has butchered a play in the field—which doesn't happen very often—he is likely to come back to the dugout muttering, "Butcher, get yourself a cleaver."

With the Detroit fans, Cash probably rated as the number two glamour boy last year, behind handsome, blue-jowled slugger Rocky Colavito. Still, this was a lofty standing for a man who had been only a part-time player the year before. In just one season as a regular, Cash leaped past such long-time Tiger favorites as Al Kaline, Frank Lary and Jim Bunning. There was hardly a day at Tiger Stadium when a group of fans with a sign labeled STORMIN' NORMAN did not turn up in some sector of the stands.

In addition to having become a sensational hitter, Norm Cash is a crowd-pleasing type of ballplayer. He performs with the pride of a professional, the determination of a collegian and the exuberance of a small boy. When he gets an important hit, he claps his hands in elation; when he makes an important play, he jumps for joy.

Before stepping into the batter's box, Cash twirls two bats above his head as though they were broomsticks. This show of strength has come to be his trademark. Norm admits that he does it mainly for its possible psychological effect on the pitcher.

When Cash got off to his great spring last year, pitchers began testing him with their own psychological weapon, the "brush-back" pitch. Norm was hit on the arms, the back and the legs, and narrowly missed being hit on the head.

A climax was reached in late June in a big series at Cleveland, which was then in contention for the pennant. In the opening game Friday night, during which Cash contributed a couple of base hits to a Detroit batting show, Barry Latman of the Indians hit him with a pitch. Umpire John Stevens ruled that Latman had deliberately thrown at Cash and fined the pitcher $50.

Detroit manager Bob Scheffing rested Norm for the remainder of that game, but on Saturday afternoon Cash was back to hit a homer that helped the Tigers win a close one, 5-4.

The series concluded with a Sunday doubleheader. In the first game Cleveland pitcher Bob Allen threw a ball behind Cash and drew a $50 fine from umpire Larry Napp. But Cash kept right on swinging. By the end of the afternoon he had collected three home runs and a single.

Another Indian pitcher, Gary Bell, told Norm after the season, "We had to find out if you were 'for real.'" The answer obviously was yes.

Before the 1961 season about the only person who seemed to sense that Norm was capable of becoming such a menace was the new Detroit manager, Bob Scheffing. In 1960, first under Jimmy Dykes and then under Joe Gordon, Cash had alternated at first base with Steve Bilko. All together, he got into 121 boxscores and wound up with the journeyman batting figure of .286.

In view of this, the prediction Scheffing made for Cash during 1961 spring training at Lakeland, Florida, sounded like sheer fantasy. It came on the day annually set aside for the special benefit of cameramen. A crew of newsreel photographers took shots of Kaline, Colavito and some of the other Tigers. Scheffing watched in silence.

As the camera crews were packing to leave, he said, "You know, you forgot one guy—maybe the best hitter of them all."

"Who's that?" asked one of the photographers.

"Number 25 over there," Scheffing replied, nodding toward Cash.

"Who's he?"

"Oh," said Scheffing, "he just might be the next American League batting champion."

The Detroit manager, who is one of the most modest men in the Western Hemisphere, says now, "Putting Norm in the lineup every day was no stroke of genius on my part. I just looked up his record in 1960 and saw that he hit eighteen homers in 353 times at bat. I figured he could hit twice that many if he played all the time."

Although Scheffing was confident that all Cash needed as a hitter was the chance to play regularly, he wasn't satisfied with Norm's defensive work at first base. So Cash daily took ninety minutes of extra practice with Phil Cavaretta, an outstanding first baseman in his own day.

The improvement in Norm's fielding was noticeable, but hardly as spectacular as his upsurge at the plate. For a time it appeared that Cash might lead the league in all three major hitting departments—batting average, home runs and runs batted in.

During the month of June, for example, he cracked fifteen homers. One of them, hit at Tiger Stadium on June 11, off Washington pitcher Joe McClain, cleared the ninety-four-foot-high roof of the right-field pavilion, which is 325 feet down the line from home plate. Only two other hitters ever did this—Ted Williams once and Mickey Mantle three times.

In the last half of the season Cash's power-hitting leveled off, but he maintained his high average to the end, never having a slump of more than brief duration.

The worst letdown for Cash, and for the Tigers as a whole, came during the first weekend in September. Detroit invaded Yankee Stadium only a game and a half behind the New York club, with a chance to move into first place by sweeping a three-game series. Instead, the Yankees took all three to knock the Tigers out of the race.

Cash produced only a meaningless single in the first game—he could have won it with a single at another stage. In the second game he was hitless. He finally came through with a home run and double in the finale, but this wasn't nearly enough to keep the Yanks from winning again, 8-5.

Norm Cash last year had to adjust to the new experience of being a marked man on the ball field. He also found himself under unaccustomed pressure away from the park. At home in Detroit, his new prominence brought kids trooping to his house on foot, on bicycle and in cars with their parents. Cash, who has no children of his own, obligingly answered all their questions and requests for autographs, although they literally rang his doorbell from dawn until dusk.

Similarly he was swamped with invitations to make personal appearances. Fearful of giving offense, he accepted as many as he possibly could, whether for fees or gratis.

One night in August when Cash was taking infield practice before a home game his vision suddenly became blurred.

"I can't see. I can't see," he said, as he stumbled to the dugout. He was led to the Tiger training room, where the club physician, Dr. Russell Wright, took over.

Cash was as white as the towel he was holding. "What is it, doc?" he kept asking as the physician examined him.

The diagnosis was an unusual one: Cash had a virus, which had invaded his fatigued body and settled behind his eyes.

Norm that afternoon had made appearances at opposite ends of Detroit. First he appeared at a bowling alley to sign autographs, then rushed to a pizza restaurant to preside at a drawing for a color TV set. After that he hustled home, hurried through dinner and reached the ballpark just as practice was starting.

Fortunately, the virus attack caused him to miss only one game. "All that running just caught up with me," Norm says now. "I'll never do it again."

Manager Scheffing declares, "He didn't know how to say 'no.' That's why he didn't hit as well at home as he did on the road"—the figures were .331 and .388, respectively. "He didn't get enough rest."

Although Norm has found it necessary to hold down his extracurricular activities, he remains as amiable as ever when he does come into contact with his public.

During the Christmas-shopping season last year a toy baseball game bearing his name went on the market in Detroit. Cash flew in from Texas to help promote sales. He appeared in the toy departments of six large stores, and ran a strong second to Santa Claus as a drawing card.

At one store a pair of teenage girls approached him cautiously. One looked about fifteen and the other about thirteen.

"Do you know Vic Wertz?" the older girl asked hesitantly.

"Yes, I do," replied Cash.

"We have the same name as him. Wertz. My name is Mary and this is my sister Nancy."

"It's nice to meet you," said Cash.

The older girl held a pad and pencil in her hand. Her cheeks reddened as she said, "Mr. Cash, I'm a journalism student at our high school, and Mr. Cummins—he's our journalism teacher—he wanted us to interview somebody important this weekend, and I can't think of anybody more important than you."

"I'll be glad to help any way I can," said Cash.

"Gee, that's swell. But . . . I don't know what to do."

The younger girl poked her sister in the side and said, "You're supposed to ask him questions, silly."

"I tell you what," said Cash. "Why don't you stand over there and listen to what the people ask me? They ask some pretty good questions."

"That's a good idea," the older girl said eagerly. She and her sister moved to one side and a small, somber-looking boy of about ten stepped up to the counter. He placed a piece of paper in front of Cash.

Norm signed his name, then playfully pulled the boy's hat down over his eyes.

The youngster broke into a wide grin. "Golly, thanks a lot," he said. He hurried off calling to one of his friends, "Hey, did you see that? Did you see what Norm did?"

Among ballplayers Cash has the same lighthearted, easy manner. He is probably the number one singer on the Tigers in the sense that he does the most singing—although not necessarily the best. Cash will burst into song anywhere—on planes, on buses, on the bench and even on the field during practice. It never matters to him whether anybody joins in; he's just as happy singing alone as with a group.

To remain a Detroit hero, Norm Cash must prove this year that he belongs permanently up there with the top hitters. Manager Scheffing, who called the turn on Cash in 1961, is more cautious now.

"Nobody expects Norm to hit .361 again," said Scheffing not long ago. "He had a fabulous year, the kind you seldom see twice in a row. But he's a good hitter, a solid hitter, and it was no fluke that he won the batting title.

"He's the most intelligent hitter on our team. He knows more about the other pitchers than any of our players. He's capable of hitting between .325 and .340 this year, and you can bet he'll be above the .300 mark for a lot of years to come."

Cash himself says with typical candor, "I've never had much trouble hitting. I'm lucky. I swing down on the ball. They say that's the best way to do it. It takes some guys years to learn it. With me it comes natural.

"I try to hit off the fastball, the way Ted Williams used to do. Let's say a pitcher has four kinds of pitches. Most of them do. You can't get set for all of them. So I get ready for the fastball. Then if he throws a breaking ball—a curve or a slider—there's a chance to get your bat around and hit it some place. But if he throws a fastball and you're looking for a curve, you're dead. You can't hit what's already in the catcher's glove."

This is a mature philosophy of hitting for a young man who came into professional ball with comparatively little experience. In fact, until he got to junior college, Cash had never played a regulation game of baseball—only softball.

Norm Cash was born on November 10, 1934, in the little Texas village of Justiceburg. He was the older of two sons of Bandy Cash, who owned a farm outside the town.

"My dad's life was hard work and my job was to help him," Norm says. "We had 250 acres of good, fertile land, and we grew cotton on two hundred acres of it. I can remember driving a tractor from the time I was ten. Some days I'd drive it ten or twelve hours."

Cash went to high school in Post, Texas. There was no baseball team but he played well enough on the football team to win a scholarship to San Angelo Junior College. Here he met his wife, Myrta Bob Harper, an attractive, likeable girl from Eldorado, Texas.

The junior college didn't have a baseball team either, but Norm and some of the other students formed an independent team in a local league. Meanwhile his football carried him on to Sul Ross State College, where, as a junior in 1954, he gained more than 1500 yards rushing. The

Chicago Bears laid claim to him a whole season in advance, picking him in the thirteenth round of that year's player draft.

The Bears never got a chance to negotiate with him, because Cash decided to be a baseball player instead. In 1955 he signed with the Chicago White Sox, who gave him no bonus but did offer a major-league contract, meaning that he was guaranteed minimum big-league wages to start.

Norm broke in as an outfielder with Waterloo, Iowa, in the Three Eye League in 1955, hitting .290 in ninety-two games. He played at Waterloo again in 1956 and boosted his average to .334.

Throughout 1957 and part of the 1958 season Cash was in the Army, where he played service ball at Fort Bliss. He accumulated enough leave time to take twenty-six days of spring training with the White Sox in 1958.

Cash says that he literally was a guy named Joe to Chicago manager Al Lopez in those days. "When I had to go back, I went up to Lopez at the batting cage and thanked him for the opportunity to train with the White Sox. He just glanced at me and said, 'Good to have you down here, Joe.'"

However, when Cash got out of the Army during the summer, the White Sox promoted him to Indianapolis and then brought him up to Chicago in September. After the season ended, Lopez called Norm into his office and suggested that he play winter ball in Venezuela and try first base, because his arm wasn't good enough for the outfield.

Cash stayed with the White Sox during their pennant-winning season of 1959, but was on the bench most of the time, hitting .240 in fifty-eight games. In December club president Bill Veeck, who didn't like Cash's "wooden swing," sent him to the Cleveland Indians as part of a seven-player trade.

In 1960 spring training Cash didn't impress Frank Lane, then general manager of the Indians. A week before the season opened Lane traded him to Detroit for Steve Demeter, a third baseman who was to last only briefly in Cleveland.

Lane dealt with Rick Ferrell, assistant to Detroit president Bill DeWitt—now at Cincinnati. "I'll give you Cash for Demeter," Lane said.

"Norman Cash or cold cash?" asked Ferrell.

"Norman."

"All right. If Bill gives his okay, it's a deal."

Norm has been better than money in the bank to the Tigers, and he is beginning to cash in himself. His 1961 pay was only $13,000, but he added about $5,000 in outside earnings. This year his playing salary has more than doubled—he signed for an estimated $29,000. After a hot-and-cold spring exhibition performance, he gave early evidence that he hadn't lost his touch by hitting two home runs against the Yankees in the third game of the regular season.

Back home in Texas, where Norm and his wife live during the off-season on the ranch of her father, S. D. Harper, Cash maintains a herd of cattle in partnership with his father-in-law. Norm aims eventually to have his own ranch. If he can keep on hitting those round white balls the way he has been doing, eventually will be very soon.

Among fans old enough to remember, few Detroit teams compare to the 1968 world champions. Kaline, McLain, Lolich, Freehan, Cash, Horton, Northrup, Stanley—their names remain among the first tier of Motor City sports heroes. Much has been written about the stars of '68, but this story, by a reporter for an enemy daily, the St. Louis Post-Dispatch, *offers a different and entertaining perspective. It appeared days before the World Series opened.*

1968

Jack Rice

TAME TIGERS

The Detroit Tigers baseball players should be every sweet grandma's favorite in the World Series. Such nice, quiet, conservative young men. It would seem unlikely that they could be rude to the Cardinals and beat them.

My first sight of them, in a group, was in the lobby of the Shoreham Hotel in Washington, D.C., a week ago today. It was Sunday morning and they were assembling to board a bus for the stadium, and an afternoon ball game. I had come to join them on the road, to watch them in games at Washington and Baltimore and appraise what it was that made them so fierce, so efficient, in winning the American League championship.

Well, there they stood, looking as if they were on their way to Sunday services, and dressed for the occasion. The only man among them dressed to wake up the congregation

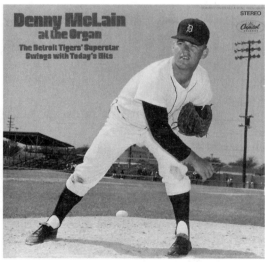

Denny McLain at the Organ, an album released in 1969

108

if he passed the collection plate was Dennis McLain, the world's premier pitcher of a baseball, by this year's reckoning.

McLain's record, as of that Sunday morning, was thirty-one victories and five defeats, and there hadn't been the likes of that since Dizzy Dean in 1934. McLain was glittering a little in an iridescent suit, Mediterranean blue. His trousers were cuff-less but the cut of the suit was not extreme. His only competition was Tom Matchick, a shortstop.

Matchick wore dark slacks and a jacket with a muted pattern, but his shirt was pale purple, a color that took offense at his red hair. However, Matchick is a rookie, and after ripening will become subdued and better adjusted to the Tiger tone.

The matter of appearance was vital for reasons of comparison. Beginning Wednesday at Busch Stadium, there will be nothing but comparisons made by the Cardinals and the Tigers, among themselves. Now, as Gen. Doubleday said, street clothes do not make the baseball team, but the Cardinals have been working all season on the premise that it helps.

They have as fine a collection of Nehru jackets, medallions, turtleneck sweaters and other mod refinements as is available anywhere among the moneyed class, professional athletes. They also could step out of their league and present a strong representative in a campus competition for most lovely sideburns.

So, looking at the Detroit men in the Shoreham lobby, the thought occurred that the series could be made a shambles. If these conservatives before me were so unlucky as to get a good look at the Cardinals as the Cardinals arrived at the ballpark in their street clothes, the Tigers would be so dazzled, so blinded, that it would take three innings for them to recover and bye-bye opening ball game, perhaps bye-bye series. Shock, and its aftereffects, could remove the competition.

I have been with the current Cardinal team, too, when it was traveling, and have ridden from hotels to ballparks with them on chartered buses. The last time I was aboard a bus with the Cardinals the echoes they left in it were louder than anything heard on the Detroit bus. I do not mean that the Tigers were tired or bored this fine Sunday. They talked and occasionally laughed, but the volume wasn't much; a man could sleep through it in the parlor of the Racquet Club.

Seated at the front of the bus with Charles Creedon, traveling secretary, I made the start on a log of days spent among the Quiet Ones, and it is as follows:

Creedon is a tall, bald man, looks sixtyish, has the calm assurance of a successful corporation lawyer, or of a good traveling secretary. Bus scheduled to leave at noon. At 12 o'clock looks at watch, says to bus driver, "Let's go." Manager Mayo Smith not on board. Am not surprised that bus leaves without him. Smith expects it to, knowing Creedon. In the upper echelons of traveling secretaries, promptness is among the prime virtues and a bus scheduled to depart at noon waits only for something important, like a flat tire.

Creedon remarks that the Cardinals are to tour Japan after the World Series. "Lucky Cardinals," he says. The Tigers made the trip in 1962. Says that only Norm Cash, Al Kaline and Dick McAuliffe, of all the Japan tourists of 1962, still are with the team. Looks nostalgic for a moment, shrugs it off.

In the clubhouse, the Tigers bring in the quiet with them from the bus. Some dress quickly, some dawdle. One of the quick is Gates Brown, a power in the making of a championship with his pinch-hitting. Brown is a smiling, assured, shuffling man, and he is shuffling toward a table where there is a bottle of aspirins. He helps himself to several and explains that he has the club cold.

The colds, he said, were brought on by champagne. Unhealthy stuff, champagne. There should be some other way to wash down the winning of a pennant. His theory is that the week before, when the Tigers secured the pennant and retired to the clubhouse for the ritual of dousing each other in champagne and in the showers, and then went into the cold night air, they got the blahs en masse.

Willie Horton, a big man in the winning of the pennant, led the team in cold content. Had to miss this trip, was hospitalized in Detroit.

Quiet is shattered. Cash does it. Puts his hands to his mouth and produces an animal sound, an imitation of something, maybe the keynote speaker at a convention of seals. Kaline looks at him and smiles. Kaline is playing his sixteenth season with Detroit, Cash his eighth, and there is between them a relationship similar to that between Stan Musial and Red Schoendienst when they were playing for the Cardinals.

Reporters come in, head for McLain. He is ready for them. Has his prop, a can of soda, at hand. Drinks so much of the stuff he should exhale bubbles. Reporters know that McLain will give them a line, and he does.

"I've lost so many contact lenses this season," he said, "and have spent so much time on my hands and knees looking for them that I look like a perpetual one-man crap game."

Manager Smith comes in. He had been detained at the hotel, grand-strategy stuff with unidentified nabobs on World Series plans. Smith is a sturdy six-footer, balding, has a deep voice, habit of saying, "That's right—that's right—that's right," quickly after making a point. Leaves no doubt he also can be quick to say, "That's wrong." Sample of firmness occurs later when he discusses with a *Post-Dispatch* photographer his conditions for allowing pictures to be taken in the Detroit clubhouse.

"No gag pictures," Smith says. "I don't like them." Photographer says he doesn't either, doesn't stoop to such things. "That's right—that's right." Dropped one "that's right."

I follow Brown out of the clubhouse toward the dugout. Can't keep up with him. Strange how the big man's shuffle gets him ahead so quickly. He goes up dugout steps, onto field, saying to others in dugout, "C'mon, we got to get ready for the World Series." Obviously in a hurry himself. Top two buttons of shirt, pants cuff down almost to shoe tops, the way boys wore their corduroy knickers in the 1930s. Notice, however, that when game starts he has tidied up.

Game itself not so tidy. Detroit has won eleven consecutive games prior to today, and Smith is using this one to keep three relief pitchers in practice. Assigns them to pitch three innings each.

Washington assigns one, Camilo Pascual. He's more than enough. The Senators look like the champions, hitting home runs for themselves, and when the Tigers are at bat, making bare-hand stops, climbing fences to bring down far-hit baseballs. Tigers don't look bad, merely pedestrian, like last-place team finishing the season and rather wistful, wishing they could have done better by themselves.

Clubhouse is quiet. Apparently the Tigers wanted that twelfth consecutive victory, a point of pride. Nobody in a hurry to leave. Smith has a theory about leaving at leisure after a game.

A New York sportswriter is quoting Gil Hodges, manager of the Mets: "A guy who's quick getting out of the clubhouse after a game pretty quickly gets out of the major leagues, too." Smith goes into a string of "that's rights," adds, "There's always something worth talking about among yourselves, some play that went right or one that went wrong, and why it was, either way, something worth hanging around to discuss. It ought to be an hour or so before you leave, win or lose."

Conversation then went into, of all things, parental permissiveness. New York writer returned to Hodges as good example. Recalls that early in the season, after playing at Houston, a half dozen Mets players boarded an airplane wearing sombreros, looked like yippie cowboys. Hodges told them he couldn't control their garb when at home, but when traveling in his company they'd do wisely to dress quietly. End of sombreros, and whatever else.

Smith nods. Doubt that group lecture would be his style. He has reputation for dealing with men singly. Noticed before game that he covered the field well, going from man to man, a comment here, another there. His manner goes with his somewhat bank-president appearance, as though he stands ready in his dealings with the players to approve any application for a loan, real kindly, but demanding full collateral as he extends credit.

Bus ride from stadium to hotel begins quietly but eruption occurs in back of us after about five minutes. Eruption is a monologue delivered in a Boston accent. Monologuist is a Miami Beach policeman, a former professional boxer, who for several years has taken vacation time and accrued leave time to attach himself to Tigers as a volunteer batting practice catcher.

Monologue is not acceptable for Sunday reading. Might go over mildly well in a Miami Beach nightclub, a small one, at edge of town. Detroit players a moderate audience, laugh at right places in most of routine, boo some of it.

At the front of the bus, Smith's mouth twitches a few times, but usually he keeps a straight face, indicates his morale after defeat doesn't need this therapy. Creedon turns his back on it, stares at road ahead. The traveling secretary plainly is not amused.

Players get off bus and scatter. Remarkable how more than two dozen men can vanish in so many directions. It is one indication of the letdown feeling the game effected.

A later conversation states the case. A pitcher, Don Lasher, says that he wishes the club could take off the weekend before the World Series, asks, "Why can't we forfeit those last three home games?"

Brown tells him, "It's ten grand, maybe $15,000. I don't know, something like that every game you forfeit."

Someone suggests a clubhouse collection to buy a forfeit. Lasher declines, says, "On my salary, I couldn't afford a half an inning."

The team's senior members, Kaline and Cash, agree that the last week of the regular season needs to be done away with quickly to get on to the series.

Kaline looks surprised at himself. Then smiles, says, "But I imagine the Cardinals feel the same way."

Copyright 1968, St. Louis Post-Dispatch. *Reprinted with permission.*

Mickey Lolich, overshadowed throughout the 1960s by teammate Denny McLain, ranks among the top Tigers pitchers of all time. No Tiger has pitched more shutouts, struck out more batters, or started more contests than Lolich. He remains one of only four men to win at least two hundred games in a Detroit uniform. (Hal Newhouser, Hooks Dauss, and George Mullin are the others.)

1972

John Devaney

THE PRIDE WITHIN

The big-bellied pitcher shambled into the clubhouse. He glanced at the clock on the wall. An hour until game time. Just about right. The pitcher liked to come to the park late when he was working. He didn't like to hang around and start thinking. Watching batting practice, he might see that his team wasn't hitting and the other team was zapping the ball pretty hard, and that was just something else to worry about when he had enough things to worry him.

Like a dead arm. He couldn't seem to get any real velocity on his slider. He'd pitch all right for five or six innings and then his arm would go dead, the velocity gone. But he wasn't surprised. He'd told people ahead of time: "The wear and tear on my arm is going to show this spring." Last season he had pitched in 376 innings, more than anyone since Grover Cleveland Alexander fifty-five years ago. He'd won twenty-five games (while losing fourteen) for a second place team, striking out 308, the most in the majors. He'd started forty-five times, at least

Mickey Lolich and Billy Martin

once every four days, and finished twenty-nine times, more than anyone else in the American League. And what had it gotten him? More money, sure, but he still wasn't making the money that Denny had made here in Detroit. And Vida Blue won the Cy Young Award. That still rankled. But today he had to pitch and his guts were rumbling. Maybe he had the flu. In this business, Mickey Lolich thought to himself, you can't call in sick. The thought made him grin.

The writer walked across the carpeted clubhouse to say hello to the pitcher. "I was just talking to Paul Foytack," the writer told Mickey Lolich, pointing to the former Tiger pitcher. "He told me that when he played in Japan there was a guy who pitched 1,200 innings over three years. The fourth year he couldn't throw the ball to home plate."

Lolich, drawing on a cigarette, winced. "Funny story," he said, his voice purposely flat. "Heh, heh, heh." He pulled off a blue sport shirt. He was wearing a T-shirt with the name *Kawasaki* printed across it. Lolich owned three Kawasaki motorcycles, the writer discovered. Mickey Lolich, motorcyclist. When the writer had been told he was going to Detroit to interview Lolich, he'd said to an editor, "Oh, yeah, Lolich, he flies the airplanes." Wrong. It had been Denny McLain who was famous for flying airplanes. Well, only half-wrong. There was a time when Mickey Lolich had flown airplanes. But hardly anyone knew it. Just as few outside Detroit knew about all those innings that Lolich had pitched last season. Curious, the writer thought, how . . . Recognition will run away from some men as though they had bad breath. Even when Mickey Lolich won three games in the 1968 World Series and was picked the Series MVP, it was McLain, McLain, McLain who got all the attention that winter, playing in nightclubs in Las Vegas, signing for close to $100,000 while Lolich was being paid half that. In 1971 Lolich won twenty-five games but Recognition skipped right by him to kiss a kid named Vida Blue who won seventeen games in the first half of the season and only seven in the last half. Vida Blue was the Cy Young Award winner and Mickey was second man again. Yesterday the writer had arrived at the Detroit airport, picked up a paper and there was a big story on the sports page . . . about Mickey Lolich pitching the Tigers to first place in the AL East? No, sir. The story was about a guy named Denny McLain pitching in the minor leagues.

Lolich was pulling on a baseball shirt. An enormous pink balloon of flesh quivered over his belt, a potbelly you see on fifty-year-old pitching coaches but never on starting pitchers. Lolich is six foot and weighs 215 and looks heavier. "I need extra weight because I sweat a lot and lose

seven or eight pounds in a game," he said in his even, soft-voiced manner. "I've had the pot ever since I was in the minors and was pitching at
Portland, Oregon, my home town. All that home cooking did it. I kept it
because I found I was no longer getting tired late in games." He patted
the pot, an old ally.

Looking at the thirty-one-year-old Lolich, the writer could understand how the jut-jawed, strident McLain got so much more attention off
the mound. There is a soft paleness about Lolich: He seems to melt into
the background. The fleshy face is shaped without a distinctive feature,
except for a curving nose that bananas between clear blue eyes. His
brown hair is swept upward to a 1950-ish hairstyle that crests uncertainly.
It is your friendly gas station mechanic's face.

What seemed distinctive about Lolich, the writer noted, were his
upper arms, huge even for a pitcher. But they seemed to be without muscle, as bloated as fire hoses. He really does have a rubber arm, the writer
said to himself.

Lolich was talking about all the innings of pitching he had done for
the Tigers. "Except when I was on military duty," he said, "I've pitched
my turn every four days, except once, during the past ten years."

He snapped the elastic waist of his pants around the pot. "Last year
had to affect my arm," he said. "Last year I was either good, all right or
bad. So far this year I've been all right and bad. The arm is OK for a few
games, then it goes dead. We were talking about it in the outfield the
other day. Someone said, 'Look at Bart Johnson in Chicago. Last year he
pitched all those innings and threw the ball by people. This year he
can't.' Usually in the spring I start throwing hard right away—bang,
bang, bang. But Billy Martin told me this spring to throw slow curves.
'Don't put too much wear and tear on your arm,' he told me. 'We need
you during the season.' Heh, heh, heh."

He didn't tell the writer, not then anyway, how sometimes he wakes
up in the morning and the left arm, his money arm, is numb, as though
he had slept on it. There are bone chips in the elbow and when they drift
out of place they cut off sensation right down to the fingers. When the
arm is like that in the mornings he can't pick up his two-year-old daughter. "And I got to pitch in three or four hours," he has said to himself.
"No way."

But the numbness fades away and he does pitch. By June, dead arm
or no, he was 9-3 and leading the league in strikeouts with ninety-five.
With the one-third mark of the season not yet passed, he was matching

his pace of last year when he won twenty-five and struck out 308. He had pitched 108 innings, not far behind his pace of last year when he totaled 376, only six behind the Tiger record of 382 set by George Mullin in 1904 when the relief pitcher was no such thing. His earned run average, 2.33, was much lower than last year's 2.92 and his career ERA of 3.40. If he could finish with a second 300-strikeout season, he would be listed in a class with Rube Waddell and Sam McDowell. . . . He would be slightly behind Sandy Koufax, the only pitcher in history to have three, and ahead of Bob Feller and Walter Johnson, who had only one.

"I'm never going to have another year like last season," Lolich told the writer. "I mean, coming close to a record for innings pitched that has stood since before Babe Ruth's time. It could stand another fifty years. How often can you do something like that?"

He slapped the blue Tiger cap on his head. It landed slightly askew. With the tilted cap and the paunchy figure, he seemed almost comic—a nightclub comedian doing a baseball act. The writer started to ask a question but Lolich cut him off. "This is a bad time to talk," he said. "I'm thinking about the hitters and . . ."

"You're not nervous?" the writer asked, incredulous. "I mean, after all these years of pitching?"

He smiled. "I'm always a little edgy," he said.

He walked into manager Billy Martin's office and asked for a report on the Oakland A's hitters. Martin handed him a sheaf of typewritten pages. He walked to the toilet, went into the cubicle, sat down and began to read the papers.

The writer had been talking to the Tigers about Lolich. A portrait of Lolich was forming in the writer's mind. Lolich had come up to the Tigers as a wild left-hander who struck out a lot of people but who let them linger for three-one and three-two counts. Fielders grew weary waiting for him to throw strikes. And sometimes, when his fastballs were being drilled back at him, he seemed to give up and say the hell with it.

"He didn't seem to worry as much then," infielder Dick McAuliffe said. "Not like me; I worry like a son of a gun. It seemed it was his natural personality not to worry. But he changed after he won those three World Series games. They turned him on, I think. He was out to bust his ass every day. It was like he could suddenly see the pride that goes with what he did and what he could be—number one."

Oakland's Vida Blue was warming up to pitch batting practice. He stopped to talk about Lolich. "I'll say this," he said loudly, laughing between the words. "I'm a chucker. Mickey Lolich, he's a pitcher."

Still laughing he went off to the mound. After watching him throw a while the writer went into the A's clubhouse and found pitcher Blue Moon Odom. The writer repeated what Vida Blue had said. "Vida's no chucker, he's a pitcher," Odom growled angrily. "We think he's a better pitcher than Lolich. Vida pitches to corners. He gives up fewer runs than Lolich. Lolich stays in games and gives up six or seven runs and steals a victory. Last year Vida had a lower ERA than Lolich, didn't he? I can understand how Lolich feels. But Vida pitched us into the playoffs and that's got to count in the Cy Young because we wouldn't have made it without him."

Vida Blue came in to the dressing room to change a shirt. Odom saw him. "You're a pitcher, not a chucker," Odom said indignantly.

Blue laughed. "Aw, look," he said. "I get two strikes on a hitter, I'm just trying to blow his ass out of there. I just whoosh. Ninety percent of Lolich's pitches are on the corners. Ninety percent of my pitches are right down the middle."

"You keep doing that and you won't be here long," Odom snapped.

"That's why I'm 0-2," Blue said, bending over in laughter.

He suddenly turned serious. "Look," he said, "when I have a bad game, I throw a lot of bad pitches. When Lolich has a bad game, he throws only a few bad pitches."

The writer was sitting in the press box with Joe Falls, sports editor of the *Detroit Free Press,* looking down on the old-fashioned green ballpark and the tiny figures warming up below in the cool June sunshine. "McLain was a better pitcher than Lolich," Falls was saying. "When comparisons were made between them, it was always to the detriment of Mickey. Mickey was smarter and more sensitive than Denny and it had to affect him. Mickey would not be the pitcher he is today if McLain still was here."

Falls puffed on a cigar. "Mickey is a good guy," he said. "He has a tendency to alibi sometimes when things are going bad. But he's always agreeable, win or lose, and never big-headed like some we've had around here."

The writer, looking down at Lolich, saw a different pitcher than the almost-comical one he'd seen in the clubhouse. From above, the paunch was not as noticeable. He wound up and threw without any seeming effort, blank-faced, like an automaton geared to throw only strikes with a minimum of moving parts. From above, his pitches appeared to be so low that the writer was sure they clipped the grass as they darted toward the batters. But the pitches must have been knee-high: The umpire was calling them strikes. Lolich was throwing fastballs and sliders that the writer, in his notebook, could only describe as "forked lightning." Most every pitch seemed to fork left or right and downward toward a right-handed batter's knees (the Oakland lineup, with the exception of Mike Epstein, being all righty). The first batter tapped a grounder toward the third baseman. The second struck out, reaching for the fastball in the tentative way of a man in the dark probing for a light switch. The third hit to the second baseman.

Sal Bando led off the second for Oakland. Lolich threw his fast slider and knew, when he released it, he hadn't thrown it fast enough. The ball broke flat and about a foot too high. Bando swiveled his bat into the ball and drove it into the leftfield seats. *I've seen him throwing a lot faster than that,* Bando thought as he rounded the bases.

Lolich allowed only two more hits over the succeeding four innings. The score was tied 1-1 when left-fielder Joe Rudi came to bat in the sixth with a runner on first. Rudi figured that Lolich would keep the ball inside so he couldn't punch the ball to right to advance the runner. On the mound Lolich reminded himself to keep the ball down—inside or outside—to try to get the double-play.

Lolich went into his compact motion. He threw the hard slider. He saw it hook inward at Rudi's knees, just where he wanted the pitch to go.

Rudi, looking for the inside pitch, lashed at the ball and caught it on the meat end of the bat. Lolich turned, the solidness of the sound telling him the end of the story, and watched the ball curve over the fence for a 3-1 Oakland lead. "A good pitch," he said to himself.

Up in the press box someone said, "That's the sixth homer in the last fifteen innings off Lolich. That's a Denny McLain ratio."

McLain, McLain, McLain, the writer thought.

In the seventh the A's filled the bases with one out. In the A's dugout Mike Epstein remembered what he had told the writer before the game: "We've got a hell of a team but if Lolich is one hundred percent, he'll beat us. If he's only ninety percent, it will be a tough battle." Epstein didn't think Lolich was even ninety percent.

Just like my last three starts, Lolich thought, the bases filled, looking at the next batter, Reggie Jackson. *The arm loses life in the last few innings.* But

Jackson seldom hurt him. He decided on a fastball outside. It wasn't fast enough, Jackson snapping at the pitch and bouncing the ball through the middle for a single that scored two runs. Billy Martin came out to bring back Lolich. It was the third straight game in which Lolich had failed to finish.

The A's won, 5-2. In the clubhouse Lolich sat on a stool, a cigarette cupped to his mouth, a can of Sprite in the other hand. He answered questions from a ring of reporters in a calm, relaxed way. This was his 111th big-league defeat—he had won 150—and he had learned, as he was telling the reporters, "Some days you are going to be bad and you are going to lose."

The next morning he clambered aboard a chartered jet with the other Tigers, unshaven, a blue tie crossed over his shirt, unknotted. He slid into the seat he always occupies, the window seat in the third row on the left, not out of superstition, he insists, but out of habit.

Usually he plays gin on the plane with *Free Press* writer Jim Hawkins, who nearly always wins. Now, chewing on a thumb, he sat with the writer as the plane rumbled down the runway for takeoff. The writer mentioned a story told to him by Tiger general manager Jim Campbell: How, when Lolich was a minor leaguer, Campbell had phoned him at home one winter and invited him to an early camp. Lolich had asked for a couple of extra days. "Why?" asked Campbell, surprised. "I got to take a test for a post office job," Lolich told him. Campbell exploded. "I'm offering you a big-league chance and you want to take a post office test?"

Lolich frowned as I repeated the story. "I don't know why he tells that story," he said. "I guess I'm supposed to be the typical screwy lefthander. Look, I needed off-season employment. I heard about this post office job and registered for the test. I asked Campbell for only two extra days so I could take the test. And he blew up. I had paid to register. I had studied. But, no, I had to report. Hundreds of thousands of people study to take civil service tests, but if a baseball player does, he's a cuckoo bird.

"Baseball players are supposed to be cut and dried. You are supposed to fit into a mold. You are supposed to wear suits and ties. You are not allowed to have your own personality. If you vary from the norm in anything, you are cuckoo, and if you happen to be left-handed, you are really cuckoo.

"Like I own three motorcycles and some mini-bikes. I like to drive them up the trails in the woods near where I live. It sure beats walking. Rarely do I drive a motorcycle on the freeway. Maybe a half-dozen times a season, out of the eighty dates we have at home, I'll drive the motor-cycle to the ballpark. It's no big deal. Millions of Americans drive motor-cycles. But if a big-league ballplayer does, it's not all right. It's something cuckoo. You violate the rules—not the written rules of the clubhouse but the unwritten rule that you are not supposed to endanger your career. They consider motorcycling dangerous. Millions of people drive motor-cycles safely. But if you are a ballplayer you are supposed to drive a car. That's safe. I suppose that in 1915, if a ballplayer wanted to drive a car, they said, 'Oh, no, it's too dangerous. Ride the old buckboard.'"

The plane was tilting toward cruising altitude. Traveling secretary Vince Desmond came back and gave Lolich his meal money for the trip. The writer mentioned what Vida Blue had said about being a chucker. Lolich smiled, drawing on a cigarette. He exhaled the smoke. "Up to the last few weeks of the season," he said, "I thought Vida deserved the Cy Young. He had revitalized interest in baseball; he was drawing people into parks. Then I caught up with him in victories. I was ahead of him in strikeouts. I had started more games, finished more games, pitched more innings. I was pitching more innings than anyone since people like Bob Feller twenty-five years ago. I said, 'Hey, wait a minute, I've done everything to bring myself into contention.'

"Still I knew Vida would win the Cy Young. But when I found I'd lost by only two votes that really hurt. I thought: 'If only two writers had known what I did last year, I would have won.' This spring a ton of writers said to me, 'If I'd known what you did last season, I would have voted for you.'

"Even Vida said it. I was on a TV show with him a few days ago. He said it himself: He thought he should have won the MVP Award and I should have won the Cy Young. Or at least there should have been dual Cy Young winners."

He snubbed out the cigarette. "You do something once in your life and you want the honors for it. But they schlep you by. That was what hurt inside. What good did it do me? Who was it in the Olympics . . . Bob Mathias, no, Jim Thorpe . . . he won all the medals and they took them away from him. His one moment in life, his only recognition, and they took it away."

The writer reminded him of one honor that had not schlepped by him: *SPORT*'s award of a sports car for being the MVP in the 1968 Series. The writer read to him what he had said when he got the car: "All my life it's been the other guys who were heroes while I just plugged along and tried to do my job. And now it's me who is the hero . . ."

He laughed. "I was babbling, I was so excited about what I had done."

The writer mentioned how several Tigers had said that they thought the three Series victories against the Cardinals had changed Lolich and made him a more knowing and confident pitcher. "Yeah," he said, leaning back in the chair, enjoying this, "that World Series was a real funny situation. I was supposed to pitch the second game but I got a boil on my . . ." He laughed when he mentioned the point of sensitivity. "I don't know how you'll put that. Anyway, they pumped me full of antibiotics and that made me feel sluggish. But the antibiotics also relaxed me and I wasn't nervous pitching in my first World Series.

"The first time I came to bat, I had two strikes on me. I told myself not to strike out. When Nelson Briles started his motion, I began to swing the bat. The pitch hit my bat. I saw it going out to left. I figured it was a fly ball. I ran to first but turned toward the dugout before I got to the bag. I saw the ball going into the stands. Wally Moses, the first base coach, had to tell me to come back to touch first."

He was laughing his dry, restrained "heh-heh-heh" laugh. "It was my first home run and I haven't hit one since."

He paused, recalling what he had started to say. "Oh, yeah, I had taken the antibiotics and I wasn't at full strength. I knew I couldn't throw the ball by anyone. I kept telling myself to keep the ball low, hit the corners. I was a pitcher and we won.

"In the next game I started, I was at full strength. I was throwing real strong stuff." He laughed. "Right away Cepeda hit a home run and I was behind 3-0 in the first inning. Between innings I said to myself, 'Hey, you got them out good the last time by pitching to the corners.' I started playing with the batters and we won, what was it, 5-3?

"Then Mayo Smith asked me to pitch the seventh game with only two days' rest. My arm was dead. He told me, 'Five innings are all I want from you.' When I warmed up I could see I didn't have a live fastball. I began to turn the ball over"—Lolich made a rotating motion with his left hand—"and the ball started to sink good. I thought, 'I'll nip the corners here, I'll nip the corners there.' That day, in a crucial World Series game, I learned I didn't have to overpower people to get them out. The first time I was sick and I had to use my head. The second time I tried brawn and when that didn't work I had to go back to my head. In the seventh game I was so darn tired I had to try to finesse them.

"After that I had something to live up to. I had to prove I was that good. I had to prove those three World Series games were no flukes. I had a lot of pride that I didn't have before in myself. There'd been times when I'd be going bad, I'd give up on hitters."

He lit another cigarette and blew out the smoke, looking up at the ceiling of the cabin. "You know, you'd be losing in a game, pitching bad. There'd be a couple of men on base and a certain hitter would come up, the kind of hitter who usually got a hit off you. You say, 'Hell, what's the use? He's going to get a hit off me no matter what I do.' But after you've won three games in a Series, you figure there's no one you can't get out."

The plane's no-smoking sign flashed on. The landing gear thumped noisily, the plane nosing down toward Minneapolis–St. Paul. Lolich dropped his cigarette into a receptacle. He and the writer went on talking, dredging the memory of Mickey Lolich, and both writer and Lolich were lifted away from this jet's roar . . . to a pastoral, serene childhood, birds chirping over the woods and lakes of outlying Portland, Oregon. Mickey grew up in a working class neighborhood called Slavtown, filled with Croatians like the Loliches. Each afternoon Michael Stephen Lolich, an only child, bounded out of the school with his friends and sped into the nearby hilly woods to sling pebbles, build forts, fish in the dozens of lakes and ponds or hunt under rocks for crayfish.

It was a childhood so happy that Lolich has tried to recreate it for his three daughters. Four years ago he and his wife Joyce flew in a friend's plane over the rim of Detroit. From the plane Lolich saw a house encircled by thick woods, lakes and ponds. He told the pilot to dip low. He saw a For Sale sign on the lawn. On a map he located where the house was: Washington, Michigan. He bought the house, a big brick colonial facing out onto 200 acres of bumpy countryside. He, Joyce and the girls don't stray far from home very often. Mickey zooms through the wooded trails on his motorcycles, mini-bikes or snowmobiles. He takes his daughters and neighborhood kids fishing in some of the lakes and ponds.

In Oregon he was a boy wonder, pitching his Babe Ruth team into two national World Series. The team didn't win but at sixteen Mickey was the Series co-MVP. (*Ah, even then never first,* thought the writer when he heard.) Sharing the honor was a lefthander from New Jersey named Al Downing.

Mickey was a Yankee fan. His idol was Whitey Ford. "I wore number sixteen on my back, the whole bit," Mickey was telling the writer one day as they sat in the clubhouse at Metropolitan Stadium in Bloomington before a Tiger-Twin game. "The afternoon I was supposed to sign with the Tigers—the Tiger scout was in the living room—the phone rang. It was a Yankee scout. He made me an offer. But the Tigers made me a better offer—$30,000 over three years—and I knew the Tigers didn't have a lot of good lefthanders in their system."

From 1959 through 1961 he pitched losing seasons for Detroit farm clubs—Knoxville and Durham—never winning more than five. But he threw the live fastball and the Tigers thought enough of him to promote him to the Triple-A Denver Bears at the start of the 1962 season. Mickey started the Bears' first game. The first batter was Louisville's Bobby Boyd, known as The Rope because of the firmness of his line drives. The Rope hit Mickey's first pitch right back at the mound, plowing it into Lolich's left eye.

For three days Mickey sat in a darkened room, the eye swollen tight. No bones were broken. Doctors told him not to worry: He would see normally. Mickey sat and thought about line drives that come smashing into your face. He didn't want to pitch for a while, maybe not for a long while. The Tigers, remembering Herb Score, told the Bears to pitch Lolich every four days.

"I don't want to pitch," Lolich said. He was ordered to the mound. He threw balloons, dodged line drives, finally was taken out. Four days later he trudged unhappily to the mound, was blasted again. In four starts he pitched only twelve innings and gave up twenty-four runs.

The Tigers ordered him dropped to Knoxville. Instead Mickey got on a plane and flew home to Portland, sick of baseball and thinking about going to school to be a gunsmith. A few days after he got home his phone rang. Calling was a friend who managed a semi-pro team. Would Mickey sit on the bench that night and coach his pitcher? Reluctantly, Mickey agreed.

The game was a close one. In the fourth inning the manager talked to Mickey's dad, a park superintendent, who was watching. Could his dad get Mickey to pitch?

Mickey's father walked over to the bench and asked Mickey to pitch. "I'll play first base," Mickey said.

"Why don't you pitch?" his father asked, knowing about the fear in Mickey.

Mickey looked at the ground. He said yes.

He struck out seventeen batters. After reading the headlines the next morning, the general manager of the Portland minor-league team phoned Jim Campbell and asked permission to use Mickey for the rest of the season. Campbell called Mickey, who agreed. The fear had begun to recede inside him when he was striking out those seventeen batters. He had his first winning season—10-9.

The next year, 1963, he was still trying to win his first Triple-A game, this time at Syracuse. Meanwhile, the veteran Frank Lary was struggling at Detroit and the Tigers sent him to the minors to try to get his arm in condition. "Give us anyone because he'll be here for only thirty days until Lary comes back," Campbell told Syracuse. The Chiefs sent the winless Lolich.

He won two games for the Tigers in the thirty days. When Lary came back someone else went to Syracuse. Mickey stayed to win five and lose nine.

In 1964 Lolich won eighteen and lost nine. He was 15-9 in 1965 and finished second in the league in strikeouts. He slumped the next two seasons (14-14 and 14-13). Tiger pitching coach Johnny Sain, who had made a winner out of Mudcat Grant at Minnesota by teaching him a "fast slider," tried to get Mickey to use the pitch. "When you can't control your breaking stuff," Sain told Lolich, "they're sitting back and timing your fastball."

Lolich couldn't master the pitch. He didn't think he needed it in 1968 when he was Mr. Able to McLain's Mr. Brilliant, McLain winning thirty-one, Lolich seventeen. He and most of the other Tigers were Mr. Forgotten Men when the Series began. Then Miss Recognition hurtled into his arms.

She was gone by mid-summer of 1969, cradled in Denny's lap, McLain on his way to twenty-four victories, Mickey to nineteen. Mayo Smith treated them this way. He picked both for the All-Star squad. But even though Denny showed up late for the game, Mayo let him pitch. Mickey was on time but he didn't pitch.

That year Mickey ranked a close second to Sam McDowell in strikeouts. He quickly found out that second didn't count. He asked the Tigers for the kind of money that Denny was earning and was told, "Look, you've never been a twenty-game winner."

In 1970 he almost lost twenty, finishing with a 14-19 record. The team came apart under a succession of blows: McLain's suspension for gambling; catcher Bill Freehan's book that told of favorite treatment for Denny; the inability of Denny to win when he did come back and then his suspension for pouring water on a writer. Lolich was growling openly about the way Smith was treating him.

In 1971 Billy Martin replaced Smith. Art Fowler, an old slider artist, was the new pitching coach. He helped Lolich to throw the hard slider that Sain had suggested. The pitch helped him to be crowned the strike-out king of the league in 1971 after finishing second two years in a row to Sam McDowell.

Finally, in 1971, he was a twenty-game winner. When he won his twentieth, he ordered champagne brought into the Tiger clubhouse. A few weeks later, when the Tigers were in Washington, he rented a hotel suite for the night and gave a party (that cost him $400) for all the players. "This may sound corny but I know it's right," Lolich was telling the writer. "There is only one thing that I, as a pitcher, can do all by myself and that is lose. For me to win, the guys have to make the defensive plays, they have to hit."

By winning his twentieth, Lolich had reversed his record of a year earlier, when he lost nineteen. Almost pathetic in his eagerness, he sought some kind—any kind—of recognition for what he had done. "I know Vida is going to win the Cy Young," he told people, "but do you think I have a chance for the Comeback of the Year?"

He didn't, teammate Norm Cash winning that award that embarrasses some athletes ("I didn't know I was away"). "Yeah," Lolich was saying this June, grinning. "I really rib Cash about that award."

As a twenty-game winner, Lolich was raised to the $80,000-plus salary level. The raise didn't wash away the worry that has burdened Lolich's mind since he studied to be a postal worker: What would he do when he could no longer throw with velocity? "I'm thirty years old and I know it's not young for a pitcher," he recently told *Free Press* writer Jim Hawkins. "Most starting pitchers are through by the time they're thirty-two or thirty-three because they throw so much."

Several years ago Lolich thought his future was secure as an executive for a Detroit pizza firm. But then he lost nineteen games and his contract was not renewed. "I know my name will be forgotten two years after I take Detroit off my shirt," he was saying in the clubhouse. "That's what I like about this job I now have with Rupp snowmobiles. I have a job that has nothing to do with using my name to get in to see people. Of course, I know if I was just Joe Schmuck they would have told me to start in the warehouse. But now I'm learning the business so I can do an executive's job when I am just Joe Schmuck."

He laughed, remembering how Miss Recognition had never kissed him for keeps. "Oh, hell," he said, "even now nobody knows me half the time."

He rolled over in his bed and peered at the light coming through the hotel blinds. He looked at his watch. A little after eight. He'd see Rettenmund in the lineup tonight in Baltimore and maybe Grich or Baylor. He fell off to sleep but woke up three or four times, staring at the ceiling, going down the Baltimore lineup, remembering what he'd thrown each of them last time.

He got up around noon and went downstairs for a light breakfast of eggs. He didn't like a big meal on the day he was going to pitch. Your body used up oxygen digesting the food and he figured you needed all the oxygen you could get when you pitched.

Lolich sipped a second cup of coffee. He'd won two straight games on this road trip, his tenth and eleventh of the season. . . .

That evening, warming up, he was throwing strikes with velocity. But in the first inning his pitches were coming in too high. *Maybe the adrenalin's pumping too fast,* he thought. The wildness cost him a run. In the second Andy Etchebarren stood at bat. Lolich threw a slider and knew instantly it didn't have enough velocity. The pitch broke on a flat plane and Etchebarren lofted it some 350 feet for a home run.

He didn't use the slider too often from there on, mixing the sinker and the fastball. He allowed only two more hits until the eighth inning, but the Tigers couldn't damage Dave McNally and they were losing 2-1 as the Orioles came to bat in the eighth.

Lolich got two strikes on Paul Blair. He decided, impulsively, to try to punch him out with the slider. As he threw he felt the ball slip and knew it wouldn't have the precise spin. The slider hung out over the middle of the plate, a white, stitched moon waiting to be savaged by Blair's bat. Lolich heard the solid crack and turned in disgust, hands on hips, watching the ball arc toward the centerfield fence. *Maybe he shouldn't have tried for the strikeout but, hell, you can't second-guess yourself.*

He got the next two outs and walked off the mound, behind now 3-1. During the last few innings he had begun to feel that his teammates would not score again. He was right, Baltimore winning 3-1 and closing to within a game of the first-place Tigers.

Later he sat in the empty Tiger clubhouse, the other players out on the field for the second game of the doubleheader. He was talking to the writer. His record was now 11-5. He ticked off the scores of the games he had lost: 5-2, 2-0, 2-1, 4-2, 3-1. He said it had to affect a pitcher's performance when he wasn't getting runs. "You sit there and you think, 'Hey,

I'm going to get beat,'" he said. "It has to take something away from your confidence."

He was chewing on his thumb. He stopped and stood up, suddenly brightening. "But what the hell," he said, "I'm not getting the hell kicked out of me."

In his next start he pitched with only two days' rest and beat the Yankees, 5-2. Then he started with three days' rest and shut out the Orioles, 2-0, moving the Tigers two games in front in the AL East. He led both leagues with thirteen victories and the season was not yet half-over.

The victory over the Orioles had been his 304th big-league start, his 105th complete game. Somewhere in that game, the writer calculated, Lolich's left shoulder had absorbed the shock of his four-millionth-plus big-league pitch. Each pitch tears tissue and stretches muscle, muscle and tissue never again the way their creator had made them. One day—maybe the day has come—a smidgin will be gone from the velocity of Lolich's fastballs and sliders and they'll hang flat and miss the corners and Lolich will retire to sell snowmobiles. He knows this will happen and accepts it with equanimity. But inside him there is a scream that echoes in the cabinet of his mind, a scream that cries out for someone to know him more than half the goddam time.

No Tigers player—perhaps no player in baseball history—inspired more fan worship in a single year than Mark "The Bird" Fidrych in 1976. His career exploded like fireworks over the Detroit River and fizzled just as quickly. In his one sterling season, Fidrych captured a country's imagination, catapulting him into the national news.

1976

Dave Anderson

THE ROOKIE

His mother was shopping one day when Mark Fidrych, then about three years old, suddenly disappeared from her side.

"We found him in the front window," his mother recalled. "He had crawled into the front window of Sears, Roebuck."

Even at that age Mark Fidrych was gravitating to the front window. Monday night Mark Fidrych crawled into the front window of the ABC television network and into the heart of everybody who watched him. Mark Fidrych is a 21-year-old rookie right-hander for the Detroit Tigers with an 8-1 won-lost record, a rock-star hairdo and a "You Know Me, Al" manner. If he were a racehorse, he would be a cross between Roger Daltrey and Ring Lardner. In a time when baseball has come to mean Charley Finley instead of Charlie Brown, some people had almost forgotten the appeal of a rookie, especially a rookie who's different.

Mark Fidrych is different. He talks to the baseball before he pitches. He smooths the mound with his hands as if he were

Mark Fidrych

stroking a puppy. He cheers his teammates when they make a good play, he consoles them when they make a bad play. Because of his natural enthusiasm, he communicates with the fans perhaps as no other athlete has. He was the primary attraction for 47,855 customers at Tiger Stadium on Monday night and after he stopped the New York Yankees, 5-1, on seven hits, he not only was cheered, he also had to return from the clubhouse to take a bow.

Part of the chemistry of Mark Fidrych's appeal might be that he's making only $16,000, the major league minimum. People not only can identify with him easier than they can with the millionaire athletes, but people also want to identify with a ballplayer who is driving a Dodge Colt instead of a Rolls-Royce.

"And he's sweating out the payments," his mother, Virginia, was saying now over the telephone from their Northboro, Mass., home. "He has a '69 Chevy, a yellow two-door, but he didn't think it would get him to Florida for spring training so he bought the new car. He's good with cars. He's always tinkering with them. And when something isn't working, he talks to the car just like he talks to the baseball. That's the way my Marky is. He's always loved baseball. When he was small, he used to go to bed with his baseball hat on and with his glove under the mattress."

He has three sisters—Paula, 23; Carol Ann, 17; and Lorie Jean, 11. Their father, Paul, is the assistant principal of a junior high school in nearby Worcester.

"When he was little, he was in the cupboard all the time," his mother said. "I remember he once poured Comet cleanser on my maple coffee table in the living room and rubbed it in. I thought he ruined it, but it was all right."

"Things are always happening to him," his father said. "In school once, he accidentally bounced an acorn into a teacher's coffee cup. Another time he rolled down a hill into a fire at the bottom. But he was all right."

"He always had a good arm," said Billy McAfee, a 23-year-old neighbor. "When we had our little backyard wars, he threw rocks and snowballs harder than anybody. But he really got into baseball after the Tigers signed him."

Disdaining college as "not my bag," Mark Fidrych emerged from Algonquin High School as the tenth-round choice of the Tigers in the 1974 draft. His antics might have turned off some baseball people. But his fastball turned them on. After the Tigers' general manager, Jim

Campbell, scouted their Evansville, Ind., farm team in the American Association last season, his advice to Mark Fidrych was, "Don't let anybody change you." When the six-foot-three-inch pitcher with the blond curls arrived at spring training, the Tigers' manager, Ralph Houk, had been alerted that Mark Fidrych was different.

"I just hope Marky doesn't change," his mother was saying now. "He sent me a dozen red roses for my birthday two weeks ago. I put one of the roses in the Bible he gave me for Christmas and when he phoned, I told him, 'Marky, please don't change.' He told me he wouldn't."

When the Tigers were in Boston last week, his mother inadvertently boarded the Tigers' chartered bus outside Fenway Park, prompting Mark to groan, "Mom, you got to get off the bus." But after he stopped the Red Sox, 6-3, last Thursday night, he drove home to Northboro, about thirty miles away, to spend the night with his family. When he arrived at The Cutoff, a small bar there, about 150 neighbors greeted him.

"One of his friends bawled him out for letting Yaz hit a homer," his father said. "He told Mark, 'I told you how to pitch to Yaz.'"

And the next noon, Mark Fidrych, the rookie who's different, was out on Bartlett Pond with Billy McAfee in a fifteen-foot outboard.

"We didn't realize we forgot to put the drain plug in until the boat started filling up and we couldn't get the motor started," Billy McAfee recalled. "Fid had his good clothes on from the night before but he knew he had to jump in the water to pull the boat back and Bartlett Pond is the muddiest pond around. So he took off all his clothes."

"All his clothes?"

"Yeah, but he took a rug that was in the boat and wrapped it around him and borrowed my belt to hold it up."

"Did anybody see him?"

"Nobody who knew him."

"That's quite a scene."

"It was an even bigger scene," Billy McAfee said, "when he got home and his mother saw him."

For Michigan kids of the 1950s, 1960s, and early 1970s, no player came close to enjoying the sustained adulation that flowed toward Al Kaline, our baseball god. These words are taken from his Hall of Fame induction speech.

1980

Al Kaline

THANK YOU

It is a great honor for me to be up here today with all these great people in baseball. But two in particular—growing up as a youngster in Baltimore and wanting to be a lot like them, or as close as I possibly could—were more or less my inspiration in going on in baseball: of course, the great number nine, Ted Williams, and Stan Musial, number six, my heroes. . . .

You know, ever since my induction last January, I've been tossing around in my mind exactly what it means to be elected to the Baseball Hall of Fame. Of course, there are the obvious answers. Whether or not I truly deserve the honor, my name always will be linked with those of the greatest hitters, pitchers, fielders, managers, and coaches baseball has ever enjoyed. That's an almost indescribable thrill and honor.

But there is more to it than that. What it boils down to is the interest, confidence, patience, care, loyalty and love of many persons—people who took time to share their qualities with me, to help me reach this greatest of honors, which all players dream of.

Al Kaline

I don't want to bore you with a lot of long lists of acknowledgments of many persons you might not even know. But if you bear with me for a few moments, you'll see that without these people there would be no way I'd be standing here today.

First, my lovely wife, Louise. Unless you're in baseball it's very difficult to understand and appreciate the role a wife plays for a player. For all the time I was on the road and all the evenings in Detroit when I was playing a game, she was at home playing mom—and mom and dad—to our two sons. For all the support when I was fighting a slump and the encouragement when I was fortunate enough to be in a streak, thanks, Louise. For all the fame and glory one derives from playing baseball, it isn't worth a thing without someone to share it with.

It must not be easy growing up and going to school while the old man is fighting a batting slump, which might hurt the pennant of the home team. But they were always there with words of encouragement, the prizes of my life, my sons, Mark and Mike.

When I was a youngster, life was a baseball game. There was nothing more exciting than a good old game of ball. I played a lot of ball games growing up in Baltimore, every day from spring to fall. I never would've had that chance to prepare for a career every boy dreams of without the love and hard work of two people, my mom and dad.

The business side of baseball has changed over the years, but I was so fortunate to play my entire career for a man—almost play my entire career for a man—whose high moral convictions never have changed. They reflected what baseball truly is all about. As owner of the Detroit Tigers, baseball and I owe you an awful lot. Thank you, Mr. Fetzer. There's another man with the Tigers who too often receives more criticism than the praise he really deserves for the difficult decisions he's made over the years. . . . The president and general manager of the Tigers, thanks, Jim Campbell.

My first manager in the big leagues was Freddie Hutchinson in 1953. Ralph Houk was my last in 1974. There were twelve others in between. I've learned something from all of them, and I respected all for the patience they showed with me. Managing is not the easiest job in baseball. Managing is the easiest job in baseball to second-guess and the hardest for which to gain respect. Thank you, many.

Regardless of what anyone tells you, a player is only as good as those other players around him. I can't tell you how lucky I've been to have played with some of the fellows I did. Maybe we didn't win a lot of pennants, but the Tigers were always there. Without naming all those who helped shape my career, please accept the hearty thanks, guys.

A young man gets an opportunity to play professional baseball only if a scout sees something in him that most others ignore. I was very lucky that the scout who showed the most interest in me happened to work for the Tigers. . . . For signing me and pulling for me all the way, thanks, Mr. Katalinas. For Mr. Katalinas to see me, I needed a chance to play and sandlot teams are only as good as their coaches. Coaching in the sandlots is a labor of love. The only reward is the appreciation one gets for seeing a few kids have a good time. So thanks to those fellows who gave me that opportunity and taught me how to make baseball a rewarding career.

Often, a player is too eager to accept praise and too reluctant to accept criticism voiced daily in newspapers, radio and TV. But without such public exposure, baseball wouldn't be the game that it is today. To the writers who voted me into the Hall of Fame and all the members of the media who displayed a special feeling towards baseball, thank you very much.

Next to my family, the friends I have been fortunate to make in Detroit and around the country are my most valuable possessions. They are too numerous to mention all, but you all know who I mean. For all your kindness, thank you very much.

Most of all, I would like to particularly thank Tiger fans everywhere, but especially those who supported me my entire career in Detroit. We've had our highs and some lows, but through it all Detroit fans have stuck with the Tigers to prove they are the best in baseball.

I was fortunate enough to spend my entire twenty-two years in the Tiger uniform. I wouldn't have wanted it any other way. Your support helped me to reach whichever accomplishments I was able to achieve. You know, I've been very lucky. In fact, sometimes I feel I've been one of the luckiest people in the world.

I've played on All-Star teams with the greatest players in the game. I was able to finish with over three thousand hits. I played on a world championship team. But most of all, for twenty-two years I was able to make my living playing the game that has been my whole life.

Being inducted into the Baseball Hall of Fame is an accumulation of numerous successes and thrills for which I'm indebted to a countless number of people. If there is one accomplishment for which I am particularly proud, it is that I've always served baseball to the best of my ability. Never have I deliberately done anything to discredit the game, the Tigers or my family. By far, being inducted into the Hall of Fame is the proudest moment of my life. You can be sure that I will make every effort to live up to the obligation associated with this honor. Thank you.

The most beloved and respected figure in Tigers history may be a man who never wore the uniform: Ernie Harwell. When honored by the Hall of Fame—a year after Al Kaline—the longtime voice of the Tigers delivered a speech befitting his grace and humility. It is excerpted here.

1981

Ernie Harwell

A LUCKY MAN

I'm very proud of this award, but I'm even more proud of my family. You know, the life and times of Ernie Harwell could be captured, I think, in two famous quotations, one from a left-handed New York Yankees pitcher and the other from a right-handed English poet. The Yankee pitcher, Lefty Gomez, once said, "I'd rather be lucky than good." And the poet, Alfred Lord Tennyson, once wrote in his epic poem *Ulysses,* "I am part of all that I have met."

Well, I know that I'm a lot luckier than I'm good. I've been lucky to broadcast some great events and to broadcast the exploits of some great players. When I went to Brooklyn in 1948, Jackie Robinson was at the height of his brilliant career. With the Giants I broadcast the debut of Hall of Famer Willie Mays. When I went to Baltimore, the great Brooks Robinson came along to replace my good friend George Kell at third base. In my twenty-two years at Detroit, it's been a distinct privilege to watch the day-by-day consistency of Hall of Famer Al Kaline. Yes, it's lucky that I've been there and I've been at some events, too.

Ernie Harwell

I want to tell you about one that Ralph [Kiner] mentioned: Bobby Thomson's home run on October 3. I felt a little sorry for my Giant broadcasting partner that day, Russ Hodges. Ole' Russ was going to be stuck on the radio. There were five radio broadcasts and I was going be on coast-to-coast TV and I thought that I had the plum assignment. Well, as you remember, it turned out quite differently. Russ Hodges' recording became the most famous sports broadcast of all time. . . . Only Mrs. Harwell knows that I did the telecast of Bobby Thomson's home run. When I got home that night after the telecast, she said to me, she said, "You know, Ernie, when they turned the camera on you after that home run I saw you with that stunned look on your face and the only other time I had ever seen it was when we were married and when the kids were born."

That other saying—I'm a part of all that I have met—I think that would have to begin with my wonderful parents back in Atlanta when I was a youngster five years old and I was tongue-tied. They didn't have much money but they spent what they had sending me to speech teachers to overcome the handicap. I know that a lot of you people who have heard me on the radio probably still think I'm tongue-tied, but through the grace of God officially I'm not tongue-tied any more. Also, I'm a part of the people that I've worked with in baseball who have been so great to me: Mr. Earl Mann of Atlanta, who gave me my first baseball broadcasting job; Mr. Branch Rickey at Brooklyn; Mr. Horace Stoneham of the Giants; Mr. Jerry Hoffberger in Baltimore; and my present boss. Here's to the greatest ever, Mr. John Fetzer and Mr. Jim Campbell. I'm also part of the partners I've worked with and there have been so many great ones, beginning with Red Barber and Connie Desmond in Brooklyn and continuing on to my present partner, WJR's Paul Carey. But most of all, I'm a part of you people out there who have listened to me because, especially you people in Michigan, you Tiger fans, you've given me so much warmth, so much affection and so much love.

I know that this is an award that's supposed to be for my contribution to baseball, but let me say this: I've given a lot less to baseball than it's given to me and the greatest gift that I've received from baseball is the way that the people in the game have responded to me with their warmth and with their friendship. Yes, it's better to be lucky than good and I'm glad that I'm a part of all that I have met.

We're all here with a common bond today. I think we're all here because we love baseball. Back in 1955—Ralph referred to this—I sat down and wrote a little definition of baseball to express my feeling about this greatest game of all. And I know that a lot of things have changed

since then, especially in this strike-filled year. But my feelings about the
game are still the same as they were back then and I think that maybe
yours are, too, and I'd like to close out my remarks for the next couple
of minutes, with your indulgence, to see if your definition of baseball
agrees with mine.

Baseball is the President tossing out the first ball of the season and a
scrubby schoolboy playing catch with his dad on a Mississippi farm; a tall,
thin old man waving a scorecard from the corner of his dugout. That's
baseball. And so is the big, fat guy with a bulbous nose running home
one of his 714 home runs.

There's a man in Mobile who remembers that Honus Wagner hit a
triple in Pittsburgh forty-six years ago. That's baseball. So is the scout
reporting that a 16-year-old pitcher in Cheyenne is a coming Walter
Johnson. Baseball is a spirited race of man against man, reflex against
reflex. A game of inches. Every skill is measured. Every heroic, every failing, is seen and cheered or booed and then becomes a statistic.

In baseball democracy shines its clearest. The only race that matters
is the race to the bag. The creed is the rulebook; color merely something
to distinguish one team's uniform from another.

Baseball is a rookie, his experience no bigger than the lump in his
throat as he begins fulfillment of his dream. It's a veteran, too, a tired old
man of thirty-five hoping that those aching muscles can pull him
through another sweltering August and September. Nicknames are baseball, names like Zeke and Pie and Kiki and Home Run and Cracker and
Dizzy and Dazzy.

Baseball is the cool, clear eyes of Rogers Hornsby, the flashing spikes
of Ty Cobb, an over-aged pixie named Rabbit Maranville.

Baseball is just a game, as simple as a ball and bat, yet as complex as the
American spirit it symbolizes. A sport, a business and sometimes almost
even a religion . . . the fairytale of Willie Mays making a brilliant World
Series catch and then dashing off to play stickball in the street with his
teenage pals. That's baseball. So is the husky voice of a doomed Lou Gehrig
saying, "I consider myself the luckiest man on the face of this earth."

Baseball is cigar smoke, hot-roasted peanuts, *The Sporting News,*
ladies' day, "down in front," "Take Me Out to the Ball Game" and "The
Star-Spangled Banner."

Baseball is a tongue-tied kid from Georgia growing up to be an
announcer and praising the Lord for showing him the way to Cooperstown. This is a game for America—still a game for America, this baseball.
Thank you.

A college football star with an impeccable build and a fierce competitive nature, Kirk Gibson ascended to the major leagues amid hype proclaiming him the next Mickey Mantle. This piece appeared a few years after his debut.

1982

Joseph Durso

THE NATURAL

LAKELAND, FLORIDA—Turn off Route 98 into Al Kaline Drive past the palm trees into Joker Marchant Stadium, and behold the phenom, the biggest and fiercest tiger on the Detroit Tigers.

P. T. Barnum isn't there spieling: "Hurry, hurry, hurry, and observe the marvel of all baseball, the flankerback transformed into a center fielder, the clone of Mickey Mantle, the one and only Kirk Gibson."

But Sparky Anderson is there spieling, and some old Tigers like Al Kaline and Bill Freehan are hitting line drives with adjectives, too. They own the only player in the world who got hit on the head with a fly ball on opening day last year, then batted .328 for the split season and .375 for the second half, and stole seventeen bases, besides.

They are announcing that the young Tigers will prowl upward through the American League's East in 1982. And they are proclaiming that the Tigers will be led by Kirk Harold Gibson, the 6-foot-3-inch, 210-pounder who runs forty yards in

4.3 seconds and once caught twenty-four touchdown passes at Michigan State before switching to baseball.

"There is no limit to what he can do," says Anderson, who learned about marvels when he was the manager of the Big Red Machine of Cincinnati in the 1970s. "He's not even close to his limit. God was very good to this man. He gave him smarts upstairs, and great ability.

"He's had to learn every single phase of this game. He never played it. In college, he played baseball only in his last year. But there is nobody that big, that strong and that fast. I don't know anyone in the game who can run head to head with him. He is the first player I ever managed with all that talent."

Then, if you somehow missed the point, the Barnum of baseball managers adds: "He is the sleeper of all sleepers. He could win batting titles. He could win RBI titles. He could win home-run titles."

Kaline, who went from high school to the Tigers and got 3,007 hits in the next twenty-two seasons, serves as one of Gibson's tutors in spring training.

"He's got a chance to be one of the great players in the game," Kaline says. "He's already come a long way. When he joined the club, he was stiff. He had football muscles, bulk, like a weight lifter. But he's competitive in the extreme. It's an unusual combination of speed and power. I refuse to compare him to Mantle yet. You're talking about one of the three or four best ever."

He pauses, and adds: "But this guy has a chance."

Freehan, who got 1,591 hits and 2,502 total bases during his fifteen seasons as the Tigers' catcher, also tutors the prodigy in camp. Like Gibson, Freehan was a star receiver in college. He laughs, kind of grudgingly, and says: "I'm from the University of Michigan. He's from Michigan State. What can I tell you?"

Then Freehan tells you: "Everybody compares him to Mantle. He got to the big leagues quickly. He's got box-office attraction. He's a good-looking kid. He got built up too soon. You put a guy in a major-league uniform, and you expect perfection, not a butcher in the field who makes mistakes. But most of his mistakes come from his aggressiveness. And he's got a charismatic personality. He can pick up a team and carry it."

Gibson, an imposing left-handed batter with soft brown eyes and a Viking mustache, discounts the commotion he is causing. He has been injured, disabled and booed while being force-fed into the big leagues.

But he also has a clear image of himself, three and a half years after he quit football and signed with the Tigers for $200,000, the biggest bonus in the club's history.

"I'm still beginning, I realize that," he says. "I've got a lot to learn. But I've got my feet on the ground."

He is asked to render a scouting report on himself, and replies, clinically: "Great competitor. Fierce competitor. Refuses to accept losing. Drives himself almost till he drops. Always seems to find a way."

The thing about Kirk Gibson is that he is 24 years old, has been in the big leagues since Sept. 8, 1979, and has not yet played a full season. In fact, he has played in only 146 games. He suffered a torn right knee in his first year, a torn left wrist in his second year and a fifty-day strike that split the season in his third year.

The thing about the Tigers is that they have not won an American League pennant since 1968. They did win the Eastern Division title in 1972, when Billy Martin was manager. But they also lost nineteen straight games in 1975, when Ralph Houk was manager. They finished in fifth place the third straight year in 1980, when Anderson became manager.

But they rose to fourth place in the first half of last season, then to second place in the second half, one-and-a-half games behind the Milwaukee Brewers and three and a half in front of the Yankees.

"The club lost Al Kaline, Bill Freehan and Norm Cash within one year when they retired," Anderson says. "Now we're rebuilding. We're the Kiddie Club. We're going with kids like Gibson, and we're going to let them play. We can win it this year."

Anderson sits on a green park bench a few feet behind home plate, his white hair glistening in the sun. He is monitoring a special workout for his Kiddie Club while the rest of the team heads across the state to Dunedin to play the Toronto Blue Jays. He is protected from foul balls and stray pitches by a screen.

It is a controlled workout, with two umpires working, left-handed pitchers firing to left-handed batters and sluggers like Gibson pushing long bunts past the charging third baseman. But at 11 o'clock in the morning, early in the week, everybody stops and turns to the east.

A few moments later, somebody shouts: "There it is." Maybe seventy-five miles away, the orange rocket rises from Cape Canaveral, and the Tigers watch in wonder as the Columbia space shuttle climbs above palm trees through fluffy white clouds. It is clearly seen here in the middle of the Florida peninsula, and the word "awesome" is clearly heard on the ball field.

It is a word that the Tigers hear often from Anderson, who ranks with Tommy Lasorda of the Los Angeles Dodgers as an optimist and evangelist. Even Richie Hebner, one of the more flip players, uses it.

"Gibby is awesome," Hebner says. "He's the only guy here who had a good offensive season last year. We saw nothing but left-handed pitchers because our power was left-handed. But Gibby was awesome."

Before he became an awesome baseball prospect, though, Gibson was certified as an awesome football player. At Michigan State, he set school records for touchdowns (twenty-four), pass receptions (112) and yards gained receiving passes (2,347). Then it came time to negotiate a pro football contract, and Gibson, at the suggestion of his coach, Darryl Rogers, developed a strategy.

"I went out for baseball," he says. "I wasn't planning on playing pro baseball. In fact, I hadn't played baseball since high school. But I figured that, if I had a good year in baseball, I'd get some leverage in the National Football League."

He got some leverage, all right. He played in forty-eight games, batted .390, knocked in fifty-two runs and set a school record by hitting sixteen home runs. The St. Louis Cardinals football team offered him a three-year contract worth $200,000. The Tigers offered him a baseball contract that started with a bonus of $200,000.

"I chose baseball," he says. "I realized the scouts were pretty hot on me. The Tigers drafted me number one. It was a chance to play in my hometown. There were advantages."

There were also disadvantages, like getting hurt.

"I went to camp in the spring, got sent down to the minors and, on the first day after I got cut, was playing center field. The guy in left field hit me broadside, and I had to take two months off with a banged-up knee.

"The next year, I opened the season with the Tigers and, one day in June, hit a home run in Milwaukee. The next time up, they threw me a change-up that I hit off the end of the bat, and I tore the ligaments in my wrist. I was gone for the season.

"Last year, I was going good, but then we went on strike in June. I haven't had a full season yet. But, thinking about it, the long layoff last summer may have helped me. It was getting hard mentally as well as physically, and I struck out eight of my last ten times up before the strike started."

When the season resumed in August, though, Gibson was flaming. He hit safely in forty-one of the forty-nine games in the second half, and twice was voted the league's player of the week. For the entire season, he hit .328 with nine home runs and batted in forty runs in eighty-three games.

But he still was paying the price of all that publicity. He was still hearing boos when he struck out, even though he was doing it less often. In the minors in 1979, he struck out once every three times at bat. With the Tigers a year later, once every four times. Last year, once every five times.

"I've been outright embarrassed, striking out so many times," he says. "There were so many bad days. But I kept telling myself: 'It'll get better, it'll get better.'"

One thing that made it better was the nonstop care of Sparky Anderson. He was like Casey Stengel carefully grooming Mantle on the Yankees or Leo Durocher motivating Willie Mays on the Giants.

"I'm a very competitive person," Gibson says. "If you dare me to do something, I'll prove you wrong. I guess I got it from my father. He drilled me. When I woke up, he had a good breakfast on the table. When I came home from school, he was waiting to play basketball. When I was down the road, he'd call me: 'Time to play catch.' I didn't always like it, but I did it.

"I suppose he wanted me to do the things he didn't have the chance to do. He grew up during the Depression and had to sell papers."

The drilling, Gibson says, gave him the willpower to survive the bad days that hounded him in baseball.

"If somebody lipped me," he says, "I'd go at him, now, the same day, like in football. I don't want to be messed with. My worst day was probably opening day last year. I lost a ball in the sun, and it hit me on the side of the head. The fans booed the daylights out of me.

"But my best day was in August against the Yankees. Rick Peters got thrown out of the game, and I was in the clubhouse when Sparky called me in to take his place. In the ninth inning, we're down, 4-2, with two guys on base and one out and Ron Davis pitching in Tiger Stadium.

"Until then, Davis had been kicking my butt, outsmarting me. But he threw me a fastball on 2-0, and I hit it into the upper deck. That's why this game's rewarding. He tried to outsmart me."

Six weeks later, on Oct. 1, Gibson hit another shot that met Anderson's definition of "awesome." He nailed one against the Baltimore Orioles that might have cleared the roof in right-center in Tiger Stadium if it hadn't bounced off an extension of the third deck.

Local historians promptly listed it with Reggie Jackson's long one in the 1971 All-Star Game and with a ball that Babe Ruth hit two blocks down Plum Street in 1926.

"But," Gibson says, "all this stuff about me and Mickey Mantle, it doesn't impress me. I don't see any similarity. I don't go for the press crowded around my locker. I'm not going to win it by myself. There's been a phenom in here before."

To keep his head screwed on, Gibson retreats into a private life away from the stadium. Although he is a bachelor, he recently bought a large old English Tudor house in Grosse Pointe. And he and Dave Rozema, the pitcher, bought a twenty-seven-foot boat that they sail on Lake St. Clair.

"Nobody can telephone me on board," Gibson says. "I've also got a golden retriever. I like to hunt, I train him rigorously. I've got a horse. I'm private. I'll come to the park and do my job, but I need time to myself."

But Sparky Anderson has plans for Gibson and the rest of his Kiddie Club.

"We're sitting on something great here," the manager exudes. "We've got kids on the way. Kids like Bobby Melvin, a catcher with super power. He's 19. Glen Wilson, an outfielder, he hit .308 in double-A, and he's 23. Mike Laga, a first baseman, hit thirty-two home runs in double-A. Howard Johnson, just like the restaurant, he switch-hits and plays third, he hit twenty-two home runs in double-A, and he's 20."

Not quite overcome by his own eloquence, Anderson beams and says: "Is that falling into paradise? All that, plus Kirk Gibson."

Ralph Houk had the misfortune of managing the Tigers during the rebuilding seasons of 1974 through 1978. Though his win-loss percentage of .450 was the poorest of any Tiger manager with at least four seasons in the Detroit uniform, Houk penciled Ron LeFlore, Mark Fidrych, Jack Morris, Alan Trammell, Lou Whitaker, and Lance Parrish onto the scorecard for their major-league debuts. Ron Luciano, one of baseball's most colorful umpires, remembers Houk in this piece.

1982

Ron Luciano

ONE BAD DAY

In 1974 I was working first base in Detroit in the seventh inning of a close game. The visiting team's batter hit a simple grounder to second base and I did the one thing an umpire should never do: I watched the ball going into Tiger first baseman Norm Cash's glove and then looked at the runner, rather than watching the runner touch the base and lis-

tening for the sound of the ball hitting the glove. Naturally, by the time I looked up, the runner had crossed the base. I figured he had to be safe.

That only turned out to be the worst call in the history of baseball. The second baseman started screaming; I threw him out. Cash exploded; he was gone. Houk put on a kicking display that would've earned him a job with the Radio City Music Hall Rockettes; he was gone. By the time things quieted down I had cleared out the right side of the Tiger infield and gotten their manager.

Ralph Houk

144

It got worse. The runner I put on first with my bad call eventually scored the tying run and we went into extra innings. I figured that was my punishment, but there was more to come. In the eleventh inning the replacement for the second baseman made an error allowing the visiting team to score the go-ahead run. Then in the bottom part of the inning the Tigers had the tying run on third with two out and Cash's substitute at bat. He struck out to end the game.

I lost that game for the Tigers. I put the tying run on base, kicked out two starting players and saw their replacements contribute to the loss. At the bottom of the official league standings there should have been an entry for "Luciano, 0 wins, 1 loss." I was really feeling dejected. I've often kidded about my umpiring career, but I was proud of my ability and hated making a mistake. This mistake was a big one.

By the time I had taken a shower and cleaned up, the other members of my crew were long gone. Just as I walked out of the umpires' dressing room, the door of the Tiger clubhouse opened and out walked the one man in the world I really didn't want to see. Ralph Houk took two steps then stopped when he saw me.

I thought, if we get into a fight, I know I can take him.

"Hey," he said pleasantly, "where are you goin'?"

"ACROSS THE STREET TO GET A #%$"&% BEER," I screamed at him.

He cringed. "I can hear you," he said, then tilted his head in the direction of the exit. "C'mon, I'll buy."

At first I was stunned. Then I wanted to kiss him. This was one of the fiercest competitors in sports and I'd just taken a game away from him and he didn't say a word about it. It was a moment I would never forget.

Houk wants to win as much as anybody in baseball. On the field he'll fight for the slightest advantage as long and hard as anyone who ever managed a ball club, but he never takes the game home with him. When it's over, it's done. He never holds a grudge and umpires appreciate that.

Excerpted from The Umpire Strikes Back *by Ron Luciano and David Fisher, copyright © 1982 by Ron Luciano and David Fisher. Used by permission of Bantam Books, a division of Random House, Inc.*

From the perspective of Tiger fans, it would be difficult to top the 1984 World Series. But over on the West Coast, not far from San Diego, famed Los Angeles Times *columnist Jim Murray had a slightly different view.*

1984

Jim Murray

WORST EVER?

Oh, well, as General Custer said, it wasn't much of a Series, anyway. The San Diego Padres are the ones with the arrows sticking out of them. And just wait till they try to put their hats on. They'll wonder where their hair went.

Take the 1984 World Series. Please.

If you missed it, don't worry. Catch the next fat-man's picnic game at the company outing next spring. Same thing.

Conventional wisdom says that the 1945 World Series was the worst. It was a mess all right. Hundreds of guys left on base (well, 103, to be exact). Errors all over the place. Potbellied guys falling down running out hits.

But bad as it was, at least it wasn't one-sided. This one was as one-sided as a plane crash.

I personally thought the worst all-time World Series was the 1936 one. The Yankees won games 18-4 and 13-5. But that was a cliffhanger compared to this one.

On a World Series scale of one to ten, this one was a one. If that.

They gave the car to the Detroit shortstop as the MVP. It

1984 World Series MVP winner Alan Trammell

should have gone instead to San Diego's starting pitchers, the most devastating strike force this side of Mussolini's Navy. Mack Sennett would have loved these guys.

They did more for Detroit than Henry Ford. In five games, they lasted roughly ten innings, gave up twenty-five hits, seventeen runs, walked eight. That's like drowning in the pool in the Olympic backstroke, sinking at the dock in the America's Cup. That's sinking to the occasion, major-league fouling-up. Detroit won the World Series because it couldn't help it.

There were times when they seemed determined not to win it, anyway. Time and again, they had San Diego in execution position but couldn't throw the switch, kept dropping the ax.

If San Diego's starters went around throwing runs around like a sailor squandering his money on shore leave, San Diego's relievers were as stingy as parsons.

San Diego's brain trust finally found a way around that. They finally found a relief pitcher to match their starting staff—Goose Gossage.

The Goose is in the hunt for Detroit MVP, too.

Consider the following scenario. It is the bottom of the seventh inning. The score is 4-3. Detroit has gone ahead on that massive power play of baseball, the pop fly to the second baseman. It scored the go-ahead run.

As the inning opens, the San Diego reliever has just struck out Kirk Gibson. Suddenly, the manager decides to bring in his all-world reliever, Gossage.

The most prolific home run hitter of the tournament is at bat. He hits the Goose's second pitch into the left-field stands. The score is 5-3.

The next batter drives the San Diego right fielder up the wall for a leaping catch at the 340-foot mark. The next guy singles to center. The next guy bunts on. The next guy reaches on an error.

Oh, it was embarrassing. But then, in the eighth, San Diego's Kurt Bevacqua, a guy who has spent a career avoiding All-Star teams, hits a home run. It is the twenty-sixth of his career, but shucks, he has only been in the game ten years. I mean, what is he, a machine?

So, the game is still within reach. San Diego keeps trying to put it out of it when a pinch-runner gets picked off base. Now, you put a pinch-runner in a game because he is (1) faster than the runner you do have, or (2) smarter.

One out of two ain't bad, but this pinch-runner, Luis Salazar, is only

(1) faster. He gets thrown out anyway. When you leave the base before the pitcher has thrown the ball, you usually do.

In the bottom of the eighth, the Goose rises to the challenge. He walks a .234 hitter. Two sacrifice bunts result in one out because San Diego throws one of them to the wrong base, one a guy was already standing on.

Now, there's a really high-level meeting. Every brain in the San Diego dugout gathers at the mound. The celebration is deafening.

The batter is a mountain of a man who has already hit a home run in this game and hit twenty-seven during the season. An unshaven bullyboy of a hitter, Kirk Gibson, not at all to be confused with the poet, Henry.

Now, when Goose Gossage is pitching and Kirk Gibson is batting, it produces a classic case of mixed emotions. Like watching your mother-in-law drive off a cliff in your new Cadillac, you don't know which way to root.

But first base is open, and stock strategy would be to put Gibson on it and pray for a double play. Or two strikeouts.

Goose gets the two strikeouts, all right. Immediately after Kirk Gibson has deposited his second homer of the game in the second deck and has put a merciful end to the 1984 World Series.

For once the Tigers didn't leave any men on base in the late innings. They blew a chance to tie the 1945 mark. They only left seventy-four. Of course, they only played five games. In 1945, they played seven.

Gibson and Gossage also did away with Detroit's chronic inability to invoke the killer instinct. Twice in this game, too, they left the bases loaded.

They might have left three again this time, but Goose Gossage would have none of it. He talked manager Dick Williams out of the notion to walk Gibson. "I can get him," felt Gossage.

So, the Sandlot Series ended as it began—on a low note. San Diego got in the World Series on a bad hop and won its only game on a bad hop. Lots of teams rely on their infields. But they mean the guys in them, not the rocks.

So, we're well out of that. In all truth, the last game was the only one even mildly worthy of the tradition. It had its moments. The others were inartistic, unexciting, undeserving of the legacies of some of the great wars of the past. The highlight film should be made into a musical. Starring the Ritz Brothers.

Domino's Pizza founder Tom Monaghan owned the Tigers for less than a decade. But he enjoyed as much success as any of his predecessors, savoring a world championship in his first year, 1984, and securing a division title three seasons later.

1984

Ross Newhan

THE OWNER

Bang the drums. Roll out the metaphors. Here we have . . . Walter Mitty? Horatio Alger? The Personification of the American Dream?

Here we have . . . Thomas S. Monaghan, forty-seven. A resident of Ann Arbor, Mich., and loving father of four daughters. A man who does 250 situps and runs five miles a day, drinks only water and juices, doesn't smoke and attends Mass at least five times a week or, if too busy to attend, brings the priest to him.

Here we have . . . lean, smiling Tom Monaghan who was reared and schooled in a series of orphanages and foster homes; earned pocket money as a youth by door-to-door selling of vegetables he had grown; attempted in vain to pay for architectural training at the University of Michigan by running a newsstand on a corner near campus; joined his brother, Jim, then a postman, in borrowing $900 in 1960 to make a $500 down payment on an Ypsilanti pizza shop, which he hoped would pay for his schooling, then

The 1984 World Series Banner

149

bought out his brother a year later for a '59 VW Beetle; lived in a house trailer when first married in 1962 and helped clip grocery coupons with his wife, Marjorie, whom he met while making a pizza delivery at a campus dorm, where she operated the switchboard, and to whom he proposed by presenting a heart-shaped pizza; and expanded with shops in Mt. Pleasant and Ann Arbor but took in a con-man partner who pushed for quicker expansion and higher profits, put all the paperwork in Monaghan's name, then filed for bankruptcy, leaving Monaghan to face 150 suits and 1,500 creditors while the government held his property in trusteeship for failure to pay withholding taxes.

That was in the late '60s.

Now?

Now the persevering and ambitious Monaghan has gone from Ragu to riches.

Now his Domino's Pizza, Inc., essentially a delivery and takeout operation, is the largest privately held restaurant chain in the world and the second largest pizza chain.

There are now 1,650 "stores," some in all fifty states, grossing $14 million weekly. His five-year goal is to have ten thousand stores doing $1 million a year each.

Now Tom Monaghan is on the Forbes magazine list of the four hundred richest Americans, with his wealth estimated at $200 million.

He wears $500 Maus & Hoffman suits, $200 Church's English shoes and, on occasion, a $12,000 Patek Phillipe watch. He rewards employees with $150 Hermes ties and Rolex watches that carry the Domino's insignia. He owns a private jet, a helicopter and a boat that he keeps in Florida during the winter and in Michigan in the summer. He will soon break ground in Ann Arbor on a $120-million, three hundred–acre complex called Dominos Farms, the headquarters for his corporation and a lasting tribute to the man he considers the world's finest artisan ever, Frank Lloyd Wright.

The central structure will be a thirty-story skyscraper called Golden Beacon, designed by Wright for the Chicago waterfront in 1956 but never built. Monaghan fell in love with Wright's work when Monaghan was twelve and borrowed a book on Wright from the Traverse City library.

Moreover, he consummated another lifelong passion last November when he bought the Detroit Tigers from broadcasting magnate John Fetzer for $53 million. Fetzer told Monaghan that the club was worth probably $35 to $40 million. Monaghan saw the chance to buy a dream and offered the $53 million. There were no negotiations.

"How do you place a price tag on something that is like a religion to me?" Monaghan asked as he sat by the pool at a Mission Bay hotel on the first day of the World Series. "I don't look on the Tigers as a commodity. I look on it as if I'm adopting a child. It's the most important thing in the world to me next to my family.

"Sure, from a business sense it made no sense. Only three clubs made money last year, and only one, the Dodgers, really made money. People cautioned me against it, but my rationale was that it would help sell pizza, and it has. Our sales are up twenty percent per store, and the Tiger purchase has something to do with that. It's given people a national awareness of Domino's and given Domino's a tremendous *esprit de corps*.

"But for me it goes beyond business. Owning the Tigers is the next best thing to playing shortstop for the Tigers. I still have to pinch myself. I still have to ask myself, 'Do you really own the Detroit Tigers, the same Detroit Tigers you were so infatuated with as a kid?' There's nothing in the world I wanted more. I mean, if I was hit by a truck today, life would have still been worthwhile."

So Tom Monaghan has made his dreams come true in a way few people ever do, and here he is, a year after buying the Tigers, in the national spotlight of a World Series against a team that came to prominence under the ownership of the man he worshiped as the guru of fast-food franchising, the late Ray Kroc, builder of McDonald's.

Monaghan first met the Baron of Big Macs in the summer of 1980, traveling to San Diego with what Monaghan said was a dog-eared, much underlined copy of Kroc's book, *Grinding It Out*, which he ultimately had Kroc autograph.

"I didn't really admire Kroc as a baseball owner," Monaghan said. "He allowed his frustrations to show. He interfered and undermined management. But as a man who knew the fast-food business, he was fantastic, a great hero of mine. I mean, here was a man who started out at fifty-one with no business-school background. He was a talented salesman who had the ability to listen to people. He didn't get bogged down in a lot of sophisticated mumbo-jumbo. His business eventually became more complicated than mine has, but I fashioned Domino's after many of his concepts and believe, as Kroc did, in the KISS theory—Keep It Simple, Stupid."

Monaghan laughed. He recalled that in the wake of their meeting,

Kroc had picked up the phone and ordered two Domino's pizzas. ("I took it as a real compliment, an indication he liked me.") Monaghan also recalled Kroc's reaction when he told him of his interest in buying the Tigers.

"He advised me against it," Monaghan said. "In fact, he nearly jumped out of his shoes and screamed, 'Why do you want to do that?' I told him like I told others that it wasn't an investment, that it was family."

The Tigers, in some measure, are the family Monaghan never had. His father died on Christmas Eve, when Monaghan was four. His mother entered a nursing school and placed the brothers in an orphanage, St. Joseph's Home for Boys, in Jackson, Mich. It was operated by strict Felician nuns, and Monaghan said his few fond memories stem from listening to Harry Heilmann broadcast Tiger games.

"He made the players bigger than life," Monaghan said, "and I knew everything about every one of them—Hal Newhouser, Dizzy Trout, Hoot Evers, Fred Hutchinson, Roy Cullenbine.

"The Knights of Columbus would take us to one game every year and it was the biggest day of my life. I'll never forget the first time I went to Briggs Stadium. The first thing I did was to look for Heilmann. He was my link.

"The frustrating thing about those years is that the Tigers never had a really good shortstop, and that was my position. The kids would call me Marty Marion. I'd still gladly trade places with Alan Trammell."

Those were years marked by little money, hard work and the ever-strict nuns. The demanding nature of those years made it impossible for Monaghan to pursue and refine his own athletic skills, but had an obvious impact on his drive and ambition.

"I always envisioned building empires," he said, "but I didn't discover the tomato sauce in my veins until later."

It wasn't until later, during a three-year Marine Corps hitch and before a futile attempt at financing his Michigan education as a newspaper salesman, that Monaghan put together his "design for life," a personal road map aimed at allowing him to realize his full potential in five areas: spiritual, social (family), mental, physical and financial.

"If I live up to the responsibilities of the first four," he said, "I can make as much money as I want—and enjoy it. I know it's not as poetic as Vince Lombardi's 'God, Family and Packers,' but for me it has stood the test of time."

The Monaghan odyssey struck a chord with the man who had owned the Tigers since 1956, the private and respected Fetzer, who followed a self-made path after his father died when he was young and who also realized a life's dream when he joined an eleven-man syndicate in buying the Tigers for $5.5 million.

Fetzer, now eighty-four and without children, hadn't offered the club for sale and had rejected inquiries until Monaghan made low-key visits to the spring-training base in 1982 and '83, developing a rapport and kinship with Fetzer, of whom he said: "He's the father I never had, the type of man I would like to be. He's a saint."

Fetzer drove Monaghan to the airport when he was leaving Florida in '83 and said: "When and if I sell, it will be to you." Monaghan: "I couldn't believe it. I wanted to kiss him." Three months later, three months of what Monaghan said were pins and needles, he got the call.

Now, Fetzer remains technically in charge as Monaghan undergoes his baseball schooling. The contract gives Fetzer and his longtime baseball man, Jim Campbell, a majority on the three-member board of directors. Monaghan wanted it that way, believing that because of his limited technical knowledge "there is nothing I can do here now but mess things up." He takes over after the 1985 season.

"If I have a concern as an owner, and I think I have the determination to control it, it's that I don't want to get so wrapped up in the Tigers that I neglect Domino's. I don't want to kill the golden egg."

Monaghan chose the name Domino's as a spin-off from Dominick's, his initial store. His logo shows a dice cube with three dots on it, which on a gambling table would mean he's crapped out.

"Friends asked me about that at the time," Monaghan said with a smile, "and I told them I hadn't even been aware of it, that I was only looking for ways to survive and that the three dots represented the three stores I had then."

He has since run the table in such a manner that it can be said of Tom Monaghan, as well as his favorite team, that they are the embodiments of the Domino's Pizza motto, which is "The Hot Ones."

Few pitchers who wore a Detroit uniform could match the intensity or talent of Jack Morris, who spent fourteen seasons with the Tigers. Morris compiled a record that earned him bragging rights as the best pitcher of the 1980s, a decade in which he won 162 games, among them this April 7, 1984, no-hitter.

1984

Lynn Henning

JACK'S GEM

In his eyes you could see the Sunday morning effects of Saturday's dramatics. They drooped from fatigue, from futilely trying to get to sleep on

a Saturday night following the single finest day of his baseball life.

The no-hit game kept spinning through Jack Morris' mind . . . the electricity flowing through Comiskey Park in the ninth inning . . . the strikeout of Ron Kittle to end it . . . the walks and the bases-loaded jam which had threatened him in the fourth inning . . . the noise, celebration, microphones and handshakes that followed amid the craziness in Detroit's postgame locker room.

"I didn't sleep too well," Morris said, dressing before yesterday's game against the White Sox. "Whenever I pitch, it's hard to wind down, so while the physical part was over by the time I went to bed, the mental part was still with me. It'll still be on my mind today."

The early-stage shock of making baseball history, of accomplishing such a spectacular personal feat, had begun to fade as Saturday evening wore on. Morris began having some genuine fun an hour or two after he had become the first Tiger in 26 years to throw a no-hitter when he vanquished the White Sox 4-0.

After the media cleared and the Tiger dressing room turned calm, Morris slipped into the training room with teammates Tom Brookens, Lance Parrish, Alan Trammell, and Tiger trainer Pio DiSalvo.

"Just to try and relive the whole thing," explained Morris.

A clubhouse attendant sent over a split of champagne, and the group toasted the Tiger right-hander. About an hour later, they rode back to the downtown Westin hotel. Morris returned to his room, called his wife, Carol, and the two talked for 20 minutes.

"She said she was so nervous she couldn't stand it," Morris recalled, half-chuckling. "I've been a participant and a spectator and I know a whole heck of a lot of times it's easier to be a participant than a spectator."

Calming by the minute, Morris and the same group of Tigers decided to do some quiet celebrating—"to have a couple of cold ones," Brookens explained.

"I was surprised how many people recognized him," Brookens said. "We didn't go more than 50 or 60 yards without somebody coming over to congratulate him. And every place we went, there was always somebody who would come over and tell him, 'Nice game.'

"It was the kind of thing he had to put in perspective—it was one win—but it was the ultimate," the Tiger third baseman continued. "Sitting in the clubhouse, with so many people asking so many questions he didn't feel comfortable. Last night, he had a chance to relax and have fun with it."

The butterflies eventually floated away, enough to permit dinner at the Oak Tree. Morris ordered a French dip sandwich and French fries. And by this time, Tiger right-hander Dan Petry had joined the group.

"He was happy, but was the same old guy," said Petry. "He kept saying it was no big deal, but to me, it was a big deal, and that's why I decided to join them (he had eaten dinner earlier). Hell, he just pitched a no-hitter . . . it was a big day in his life. You kind of envy that, you kind of want to help him live it a little. I just wanted to go out with him. I know if I had pitched a no-hitter I'd have wanted my friends along.

"They make a big deal about something like that, but hell, it is a big deal. It's the kind of thing where you say, 'Go ahead, Jack. Have fun.'"

Morris was back in his room early. Having told the hotel desk to hold all phone calls, he settled in for a night of sleep. Intermittent sleep. Yesterday morning, admitting he felt tired, Morris still was trying to sort out the swirl of thoughts.

"It's just a heck of a sense of accomplishment, but at the same time I've got mixed emotions," Morris said. "I'm the guy throwing the pitches, but I can't do it without those guys behind me, and yesterday we had at least three or four great plays. That's why guys throw no-hitters."

That's one reason. Another might have something to do with the guy pitching.

"His forkball was awesome," Petry acknowledged. "I said to Milt (Wilcox) in the third inning, 'They've got no chance.' You never think about a no-hitter at that point, but you could see he had everything going."

Morris' cap and the baseball he threw to strike out Kittle will be shipped to the Baseball Hall of Fame in Cooperstown, N.Y., a place that might eventually house Morris if this kind of thing continues.

"Maybe it still hasn't sunk in," he said, "but there was a lot of luck involved. I've had better stuff on other days, but never thrown a no-hitter, so that explains that."

Not necessarily. The flukes, the quirks of fate that all had their minor roles in Saturday's masterpiece didn't for a minute upstage the star, Jack Morris, who by any estimate threw a pretty extraordinary game at Comiskey.

Every kid who loves baseball dreams of meeting his idol. For Jimmy Shine, son of future Free Press *publisher Neal Shine, the dream became a reality when his father took him into the Tiger clubhouse in the early 1960s.*

1985

Neal Shine

ON KALINE'S KNEE

Jimmy Shine's memory of that precious day in his young life remains bright.

"I remember the clubhouse and the players getting dressed for the game," he says. "There was a guy with a box of baseballs and he was rubbing them and he gave me one. I remember taking the ball around the room, asking the players to sign it."

Rocky Colavito signed it. So did Al Kaline, Jake Wood, Bubba Morton, Chico Fernandez and Tiger manager Bob Scheffing.

"Don Mossi was on the rubbing table and when I shook hands with him, he asked me not to shake his pitching hand because he was afraid I would hurt it. So I shook his other hand. I thought that was great.

"But mostly I remember Al Kaline. He was the hero. He put

Al Kaline and owner John Fetzer

me on his lap and showed me how to hold the bat. It seemed like the biggest bat I had ever seen. Then we had our picture taken."

It was 1962, somewhat less than a remarkable year for the Tigers, but to Jimmy Shine at age six, Tiger baseball was more important that year than the order of finish in the American League.

He was, even at six, already an irretrievably committed Tiger fan, a condition that has not diminished with the passage of time.

Joe Falls, who was the Free Press baseball writer then, arranged for Jimmy, my oldest son, to visit the Tigers in the clubhouse before the game.

He missed a half-day of school, but it was to be a great adventure, something that would not be matched by anything happening that afternoon in the first grade.

Later in the stands, as the Tigers went through the late-season motions with the Angels before a small crowd, Jimmy read and re-read the signatures on his baseball through the clear plastic sandwich bag in which he had wrapped it.

Then he talked about Al Kaline and sitting on his lap and how good it was that he was going to have a picture of himself with Kaline. "I sure hope it turns out," he said of the picture.

I assured him that the Free Press photographer, Dick Tripp, was a professional and all his pictures turned out.

About two weeks later I began to hound Tripp in earnest for a print of the picture. I told him I was unwilling to go home each night knowing that Jimmy's first question would be: "Did you bring the picture?"

There was, it seems, some understandable skepticism among Jim's first-grade colleagues, who would believe that he had been sitting on Al Kaline's knee only after they saw the picture. Jimmy insisted that photographic evidence of that historic moment would be provided soon.

After about a month, Dick Tripp worked up the nerve to tell me. He had lost the picture and the negative.

Bernice Haun, who worked in the photo department and had a mother's understanding of the situation, had spent a week searching through every negative in the department. It was not to be found.

I asked Tripp if he would mind stopping by my house on his way home from work and telling my son what happened. Tripp, who had six children of his own and understood fully all that was involved in such a task, declined.

That night, in one of the shortest, most difficult conversations of my life, I told Jimmy that there was no picture. That it had been lost and there was no hope of finding it. That I was truly sorry.

He didn't cry. He just turned and went upstairs to his room and closed the door. Although we have talked many times through the years about that day, he never again mentioned the lost photo. Whatever unpleasantness he had to endure from his doubting classmates, he kept to himself.

Jimmy is twenty-nine now and lives in Bradenton, Fla., with his wife, Deanna, and their year-old son Colin. The people at the *Bradenton Herald,* where he is the retail advertising manager, call him Jim.

It's not possible, really, to go back twenty-three years and capture a treasured moment that was missed forever one day in a crowded locker room. Special memories aren't easily recaptured and trying to go back often diminishes the importance of it all.

But last month, Jim Shine and Al Kaline got together again at the Tiger spring training camp in Lakeland. They talked about the 1984 season and about the Tigers' chances in 1985. Then they stood together by the right field fence and had their picture taken.

It wasn't quite the same as that magic afternoon in 1962, but it was good and it was something worth doing.

And this time the picture turned out.

1989

Hank Greenberg

MY ROOMMATE JO-JO

I was fascinated by the people I met in baseball.

Most of the players came from rural areas—about half of my Detroit teammates were from the South—and they knew all kinds of things that I had never learned. Their whole life experience was with animals, and they knew how animals lived—how they copulated, what they ate, how they behaved. They saw the whole pattern of life in terms of animals and crops and soil, and there wasn't any situation that they couldn't describe in agricultural terms. When I first came up, I was dismayed by this, but I soon learned that the other players had their lexicon and I had mine, and one was as expressive and descriptive as the other. When they got hold of a pitch and drilled it over the fence, they'd come back to the bench and say, "Boy, I really cow-tailed that one!" A fly ball became a can of corn. They seemed to have a homespun knack for describing people, too. When

"JO JO" WHITE

Pete Fox and I got our first look at six-foot-eight pitcher Mike Wayant, Pete whistled and said, "Man! He's big enough to have two belly buttons." Only belly buttons wasn't the precise word he used. When some particularly oversexed rookie came along, they'd say he was "horny as a hound dog in heat," and this sort of remark would puzzle a Bronx boy who had never heard the word "horny" and had never seen a "hound dog" and didn't know what "heat" meant. But after a while I caught on.

That kind of talk began to come naturally, and it didn't even sound vulgar anymore. Most of our intimate nicknames for one another had to do with fornication and defecation (they persist today). The better we liked each other, the worse the names.

My first roommate was Joyner "Jo-Jo" White from Georgia. He was called Jo-Jo because of the way he pronounced his native state. And no two people could be more different than me, coming from the Bronx, and Jo-Jo White, claiming he came from Atlanta. Well, when we pinned him down, it was twenty-five miles out of Atlanta, a little town, Red Oak, Georgia, that didn't even show up on the map. Anyway, our relationship was terrific. We used to fight the Civil War every night. Jo-Jo would say, "Why my granddaddy would chase your granddaddy right up the goddamn hill and run his ass off." I hated to tell him that this would have been impossible, as my granddaddy had been in Romania at the time, but that didn't keep Jo-Jo from carrying on. He couldn't conceive of anybody coming from any place except Georgia, or being brought up on anything but a dirt farm, and he still could not assimilate the idea that the South had lost the Civil War.

Jo-Jo was a center fielder and leadoff hitter. He had great speed and really knew how to slide. I used to urge him to get on base, because I would try to drive in runs and lead the league in RBIs. One time he was on third and I faced a fellow by the name of Mickey Haefner, a short left-hander who didn't have much on the ball. The game wasn't close and there was no need for Jo-Jo to try to steal home, but he did. He was thrown out. As he was lying there on the ground, I said, "The next time you do that, I'm going to hit you right on the head with the bat." He deprived me of a good chance at an RBI, and he did it deliberately because he knew it would burn me up.

Excerpted from Hank Greenberg: The Story of My Life
by Hank Greenberg and Ira Berkow, copyright 1989.
Reprinted with permission of Triumph Books, Inc.

Cecil Fielder spent only seven seasons in a Detroit uniform, but he left his mark, leading the league three times in runs batted in and twice in home runs. In 1990, the year this column appeared in the Washington Post, *Fielder clouted more than fifty—one of which flew over the roof beyond left field at Tiger Stadium.*

1990

Tom Boswell

BABY BABE

The Detroit Tigers are hanging around the batting cage. A line drive streaks toward third base where a rookie, up for September, is not paying attention.

"Hey!" one alarmed voice screams.

The rookie lifts his foot just in time not to get hurt.

A few minutes later, another line drive. The same player is day-dreaming. "Hey!" screams the same voice, saving the same guy's life. "Don't get hurt out there now," the Good Samaritan yells cheerfully. The rookie waves back, shamefaced but still in one piece.

When batting practice breaks up, every Tiger player avoids the fans along the box seat railing, just as almost every other major league player does. Sign one autograph, a mob will gather and you'll not only have to sign one hundred times, but you'll actually have to— yuck—shake hands and talk to the fans.

Even though no fan spots him or calls his name, the same Tiger walks directly to the box seats and takes a small

Cecil Fielder topped the left-field roof at Tiger Stadium

boy's program and pen and begins the autograph session. He keeps signing for fifteen minutes until the police order him to stop and go into the
clubhouse. At one point, the player realizes that two kids in the front row
are getting squeezed by other fans. "Are these your seats right here?" asks
the 247-pound Tiger.

The children are too awed to speak, but they nod. So the player
moves down the row to prevent their seats from becoming a war zone;
also, he can answer questions from a new batch of fans.

"Did all that sushi make you strong?" asks one man, not expecting an
answer.

"Yup. I'm going back for more," says the Tiger as he signs his name
slowly, perfectly legibly—an artistic autograph in defiance of the sport's
tradition of quick, sloppy blurs.

One boy walks away, not knowing who the lone signer is. Suddenly, as
if shocked, he looks at his ball and yells, "I got Cecil Fielder's autograph!"

If you really want to know what a ballplayer is like as a person, don't
just listen to him talk. Watch him when he's around other players. Or
when he thinks nobody's watching him at all. At least that's what Sparky
Anderson says.

The Tigers manager never dreamed that Cecil Fielder would hit
forty-five home runs—nine more than anybody else in the major leagues
this season—or that he might become the eleventh man in history to hit
fifty homers before this season is over. But he knew he had a team leader
as far back as spring training.

"He has the same temperament as Alan Trammell," says Anderson,
meaning that as high praise since Trammell always epitomizes sweet-tem-
pered stability. "Players teach you about other players. Watch who they
avoid, who they enjoy being around. That's part of the way you decide
who to subtract from your club the next year.

"All the players liked Cecil from the first day. He is who he is. He
doesn't try to be liked. He's just relaxed and comfortable being himself.
We gave him about $3 million for two years. You lay out that kind of
money and you find out right away who the jerks are."

Everybody knows Cecil Fielder's story now. But not too many know
him. No player in baseball, until Fielder, had the self-confidence, or
maybe audacity, to go to Japan—at age twenty-five—to prove that he was
a star and not a part-time platoon player. In bits and pieces of four seasons with the Blue Jays, Fielder hit thirty-one homers in 506 at-bats. He

didn't rebel. He didn't call names. He just left. And became a Hansin Tiger—one who hit thirty-eight home runs in 106 games.

In Japan he learned to hit soft slop and accept walks. When Detroit had the fiscal courage to make him another kind of Tiger, Fielder had his chance. "You just got to find out who you are. I got a chance," he says. "I had a lot of things to prove to myself. And you can't do it unless you play every day and relax. You have to let things happen. You can't worry about when you'll play again. . . .

"In spring training, I relaxed a little more. When I didn't get off to a good start, Sparky told me, 'I know you're going to hit.' I knew I'd play. The people who didn't think I could play the game," said Fielder earlier this year, "they can't take this from me."

Because Fielder is so wide, so ominous at the plate, and hits the ball so far—he is the first right-handed Detroit player to hit a ball entirely out of Tiger Stadium—it's often assumed that he must be macho. Actually, he seems the opposite.

"He's so polite and has such a nice family," says Anderson. "We tease him that he must have met his wife when he was a high school [basketball] star at point guard because that's the only way he could've won her. She's so beautiful he couldn't get her now. She teases him about that too."

Of course, this may only be part of Sparky's plan to get Fielder to "come to spring training at 230 pounds next year." Typically, Fielder doesn't squawk at being asked to lose weight after one of the greatest offensive seasons in the last quarter century. "He's not real joyful about the idea," said Anderson, "but I promised we'd work it out together. Some guys can carry a lot of weight. It's a fine line. I don't want to get too smart for our own good."

Babe Ruth weighed 251 when he hit sixty homers. And Fielder is having a Ruthian season. Only one man, George Foster, has hit fifty home runs since 1965. No player, including Fielder, will admit the symbolism of fifty homers. But that magic number—achieved less often in this century than a .390 batting average—seems to bedevil even the best sluggers.

Since Willie Mays hit fifty-two in 1965, many of the greats have had a chance for fifty after Labor Day and then started to falter. Mark McGwire, Andre Dawson, Frank Robinson, and Harmon Killebrew (twice) got stuck on forty-nine. Mike Schmidt, Dave Kingman, Willie Stargell, and Frank Howard made it to forty-eight. After being ahead of the fifty-homer pace, Kevin Mitchell, George Bell, Hank Aaron, and Reggie Jackson came to a halt at forty-seven.

"If he does hit fifty," says Anderson, "you'll never know, other than he might smile once while he's rounding the bases. This guy is going to hit thirty or more homers every year, but he will be the same person ten years from now."

As Anderson talks, a small elderly Baltimore man approaches Fielder and asks him some questions. As the fellow comes back through the Tigers dugout, he looks worried. "Cecil said he would come to our banquet this winter," he says. "Last winter, we invited Jose Canseco. He stiffed us and didn't show up."

Whether he gets his fifty or not, Fielder will be there. Anybody who watches him closely wouldn't have a doubt.

*Rebecca Stowe was born in Port Huron and grew up listening to the Tigers on WJR. She is the author of three novels—*Not the End of the World, The Shadow of Desire, *and* One Good Thing—*and, though a resident of New York, still counts herself among Willie Horton's fans.*

1990

Rebecca Stowe

SENTIMENTAL WILLIE

Tiger Stadium, 1972: I'm sitting in the left-field seats with my husband and some friends. It's my first game at Tiger Stadium in ten years—I'd been too busy being a Beatlemaniac during high school to pay much attention to baseball. But I'm older now, more mature, a college student, practically a matron. The opposing team is up and the batter hits a fly ball to left field. Willie Horton lumbers after it, but he's not in time; it drops in, base hit, the crowd boos. I'm furious—how dare they? A group of drunks behind us starts chanting, "Trade 'im." "Booooo," hisses my husband, a mere hockey fan. "Don't listen to them," I shout to poor Willie, who's practically slumping inside himself he's so hurt and upset. "You just go up there and hit a home run. You'll show them!" And next

at bat, he does—he sends one flying and the crowd roars. And cheers. And screams. And Willie, God love him, comes running around the bases, beaming and happy and forgiving as a child. That does it; I'm hooked. Back in love with baseball. Willie was "my" Tiger.

I grew up in a home

Willie Horton

166

where the radio was permanently set on WJR; I thought George-Kell-and-Ernie-Harwell was one word. I'd fall asleep listening to my parents discussing the merits and flaws of various Detroit players, and by the time I was twelve I wanted one of my own, a Tiger, my very own player to root for and adore. In 1962, my goals in life were to be the first woman governor of Michigan and to marry Rocky Colavito. I was crazy about him, in love the way only a twelve-year-old who knows nothing about it can be. It was my love for him, rather than baseball, that led me to my first game at Tiger Stadium—that twenty-two-inning, seven-hour marathon with the Yankees, which the Tigers lost despite Rocky's heroic seven hits in ten at-bats: more than Maris, Mantle, and Berra combined. Seven hours was a long time for a preteen whose only interest in baseball was Rocky Colavito, but was I weary? Never. During the "boring parts" (i.e., when the Yankees were at bat), I sat happily carving ROCKY in the chest of a stuffed Tiger my father bought to keep me quiet.

Seasons passed. Rocky went back to Cleveland and the Beatles replaced baseball as my passion, even though my mother tried valiantly to keep my interest alive. "You need a new Tiger," she'd say hopefully. "What about Al Kaline?" Oh, pul-eeeze. Everybody loved Al Kaline. She loved Al Kaline. I wouldn't be caught dead loving the same Tiger my mother loved! My mangy old stuffed Tiger got tossed in the closet with the rest of my childhood. I still followed the Tigers and rooted for them faithfully, but it was mostly out of regional loyalty, during a time when practically the whole country was happily Detroit-bashing, calling it the Murder Capital of the U.S. and making other snide remarks. I secretly adored Al and, of course, I liked Stormin' Norman Cash . . . and I was kind of interested in this new Tiger, this local kid everybody kept comparing to some "Campy" guy. Willie Horton; Willie the Wonder. I thought it was great he hit so many home runs, but what was a "ribby"?

It wasn't love yet, it was more like a flirtation. I liked him because he was a ghetto kid, the son of a coal miner and the youngest of nineteen children. He was so poor when he was growing up he almost had to drop out of school because he didn't have shoes. When he signed with the Tigers, the first thing he did was buy a house for his parents. The guy had class.

Being sentimental, I liked that before his first All-Star Game, he ran around the field collecting his heroes' autographs. I also took note that he gave cookouts for the Tigers' grounds crew. I thought it was amusing when he showed up at spring training overweight and said, "I only eat two meals a day. I just like snacks." When he took off twenty-two pounds and Tiger manager Charlie Dressen presented him with a twenty-two-pound ham and told him not to eat it all at once, I could identify. It was the sixties, and while I was no radical, my consciousness was getting raised. So I liked that he donated time to work with ghetto kids, "kids who don't know what middle class means." Right on, Willie. And besides, he swung a mean bat.

I went off to college and got married, but not to Rocky. All anyone could talk about was Denny McLain and his damn organ. Willie the Wonder, meanwhile, was falling out of favor with the press and the fickle, fickle fans. The first time they booed him he got so upset he didn't show up the next day. Everyone was outraged, but I just grew more fond of him. The more they dumped on Willie, the more I liked him—how, I asked, can you not like someone who has two sons with the same first name?

Just about then, I went to that fateful game. When we got home, I called my mother with the good news that I'd found my Tiger. "Who?" she asked. "Willie!" I said joyfully. "Oh," she said after a pause. "That big baby?"

Yes, that big baby. Because of him I fell back in love with baseball. In learning about Willie, I learned about the game, something he, being an inveterate fan, would appreciate. I also learned a kind of pidgin base-ballese. "His stats are solid," I'd say. "He's horribly underrated as a fielder." "Have you forgotten that game in '69 when he tied the AL record for outfielders with eleven putouts?" "And what about that perfect throw in game five of the '68 World Series when he nipped Lou Brock at the plate?"

No one quarreled with Willie's power. In the five seasons he played more than 140 games for the Tigers, he hit between twenty-five and thirty-six homers. Pitchers were terrified of him. Third basemen backed up. He was known as both a power hitter and a power squeezer. "My ribs still hurt," New York manager Ralph Houk complained after Willie grabbed him during a Yankee-Tiger brawl, to which Willie replied, "He was lucky I just squeezed him." Willie was a one-man gang in brawls. After watching him in action, umpire Marty Springstead contended, "Willie is the strongest man in the league. Willie is the strongest man in any league."

It was true that he was injury-prone and rarely made it through an entire season. He invariably began the year leading in something—

home runs or runs batted in (so that's a "ribby"!)—but he would pull a hamstring or tear a ligament or get hit in the head. Detractors squawked "Hypochondriac!" but how do you fake knee surgery? If he could play, he'd play—this is the man who got hit by a car while chasing the team bus and got up, grabbed a cab, went out to the stadium, and played!

But did the fans appreciate him? No! On opening day in '73, forty-some-odd thousand fans cheered the Tigers as they were introduced—all except Willie, who got some jeers. Detractors called him moody, but how would they feel if they went into their offices and found forty-some-odd thousand hissing former fans stuffed into their cubicles?

He was human, but I liked those feet of clay. Every year at spring training, he'd arrive early and fat, using the "I just like snacks" routine, and when that didn't work, he'd say he couldn't help it, he had heavy muscles. (He did; he was going to be a boxer until his father saw him get beat up on TV and nixed that career.) He'd get upset when he didn't get to play and skulk off to the clubhouse, but he'd always get over it and end up back on the bench, cheering more heartily than the most vehement fan. Yes, he tended to sulk, but he'd always bounce right back and with boundless enthusiasm, come to the park five hours before anyone else, to work out with weights and practice his swing with a broom handle. (As a rookie, he'd show up for the team bus an hour and a half early to make sure it wouldn't leave without him.) When he became a DH in 1975, he'd spend his bench time pretending he was out in left field, thinking about how he'd field the ball. "I just want to play," he said. "I don't care if I have to play in the street."

The man loved baseball.

"The Tigers are my family," he said over and over, and even when they traded him in 1977, after all those years of loyal service, he still proclaimed, "I'll always be a Tiger." Yes, he was sentimental, but what's wrong with that? He had cried when the Tigers traded Mickey Lolich, but so did a lot of other people I knew.

I kept an eye on Willie after he got traded, and I was very proud when the *Sporting News* named him the American League's Comeback Player of the Year in 1979. As the DH in all 162 games for the Seattle Mariners, he hit twenty-nine homers and had 106 RBIs, showing exactly what he could do if he played every day.

He went back down to the minors after another season in Seattle, his eighteen-year major league career over, and I didn't hear anything about him again until 1985, when I was out at Yankee Stadium cheering my newest Tiger, Chet Lemon. "Horton?" I asked while glancing at the Yankee roster. "Could that be Horton as in Willie?" Sure enough; Billy Martin, the man who, when managing the Tigers, had challenged Willie to a fistfight, had brought him to the Yanks as something called a "tranquility coach."

Tranquility and Willie didn't go together. I did remember his once saying, "I just judge everybody as a human being—even umpires," but that hardly qualified him for Buddhahood. Unless the TC was just a euphemism for the guy who sits on the players when they get out of line, it made no sense at all. Unless it was a joke, it wasn't funny.

Willie was a Tiger, not a Yankee. Willie was tempestuous, not serene. It was his perturbability that made Willie so wonderful. He was human and real, not a baseball card. If Willie wasn't Willie, who was I? I longed to see him come charging out of the dugout to toss a few umpires around, or at least to pout and stomp, but nothing happened. Even Billy Martin was restrained.

The Tigers won and Chet got a hit, but I found myself pouting and stomping and wishing I could toss a few umpires around. Somebody had to be disappointed and petulant. Somebody had to be Willie.

Popularity can be fickle. When Tom Monaghan bought the Tigers in 1984 and promptly won a world championship, he found himself in the glow of public adulation. (Take a look at Ross Newhan's piece earlier in this book.) But it lasted not even a decade. By 1992, Tiger fans were ready for a new owner, Mike Ilitch.

1992

Mitch Albom

WHITE KNIGHT

It was like one of those arranged marriages in the old country. The bride wore yellow balloons and offered fresh fruits and cakes. The groom arrived in a fine blue suit and brought his family. He complimented the lady on her grace, despite her years. He listened to her sing "Take Me Out to the Ball Game" through her aging loudspeakers. For a moment, he appeared to blush, as if overwhelmed by the ceremony. He was really hers? She was really his?

"Talk about a field of dreams," Mike Ilitch said, sighing.

I have witnessed many Opening Days at Tiger Stadium. I have never seen one with as fresh a feeling as Wednesday, a balmy afternoon in mid-August. There were white tablecloths on long buffet tables—all set up in right field. There were waiters circling home plate with desserts. There were frills and gimmicks—but more than that. There were smiles and sighs of relief. It was some sort of rebirth down at Michigan and Trumbull, like the morning after Noah's flood. Everything was bright and dewy and ready for rebuilding.

Which is exactly what this baseball team needs, of course. Rebuilding. Rejuicing. Rejuvenating. Mike Ilitch—who began his new era by letting go of several top front-office people—might have worn blue for his first official day as Detroit Tigers owner, but he was the white knight to fans. And the questions from the media reflected that:

"Will you keep Tiger Stadium?"

"Will you sign Cecil Fielder?"

"Will you bring back Ernie Harwell?"

If Ilitch did everything that was asked of him Wednesday, he would need another lifetime—and maybe a couple of tablets to write his Ten Commandments. Yet he smiled, he answered the questions. He even made jokes, suggesting that he really wanted Fielder to play for his hockey team.

And in simply doing the one thing he does best—handing over the money and making the purchase—Ilitch accomplished a feat that had grown nearly impossible in the old Tigers regime:

He gave this franchise hope.

And isn't hope the basis of all good marriages?

"I dream of the day when the buses come rolling down here from all across the state," Ilitch said, sounding like a Kennedy running for office. "I dream of the day when moms and dads take their kids to a game again. . . ."

"When you first started with the Red Wings you gave away a free car each night to boost attendance," a reporter said. "Would you do that again with the Tigers?"

"Hey, if I have to," Ilitch answered, "I'd give away free limos."

Free limos. He made promises like that. He talked of winning and spending money. He talked of signing old stars and going after new ones. He said everything right, everything the old regime, under kooky Tom Monaghan, would never say.

Example: They said no more Tiger Stadium? Ilitch said he would consider keeping Tiger Stadium.

They said no more Ernie Harwell? Ilitch said he might bring Harwell back.

They said, "We'll move if we don't get our way"? Ilitch said, "I will never take this team out of Detroit. Never."

The white knight.

Now, normally, a fellow like this comes along, and the media slice him apart, as if he were a kid wearing a new suit to reform school. And yet you won't find any cynicism in this column. And you might not find it elsewhere this morning. Here is why: Mike Ilitch is a rare bird.

He actually means what he says.

And because of that, this was a fine day in Tigers history. Maybe now we can blow away that stale, crusty air that always hung over this team and bring it into the 1990s. Maybe now we can look forward to going to the ballpark—if Ilitch delivers on his promise to "make it an exciting place, for kids especially."

It is true, only hours after Ilitch's introduction party, several front-office people . . . were let go (or not offered new employment, to be technical). But hey. You wanted change? You got change. . . .

Anyhow, these changes are small pebbles compared to the biggest change: the philosophy of the owner. Tom Monaghan once said he bought the Tigers to make up for the fact that he was cut from his eighth-grade baseball team. The poor kid turned rich, ready to get back at all his enemies.

Ilitch harbors no such vindictive thoughts. He is not trying to prove his macho by buying a team he could never dream of making. On the contrary, the Tigers are a team that Ilitch once came close to making, as a minor league player in their farm system. So he is not so much buying a new dream as picking up an old one, a dream he interrupted for the rigors of real life and one he now returns to, at age sixty-three, with the same boyish enthusiasm he once showed running the bases. His former coach at the minor league level remembers him as "a guy with as much hustle as Pete Rose, a guy who loved the game."

Wednesday, Ilitch talked about love, too.

"You can do a lot on love," he said, explaining how he will balance this new burden with Little Caesars, the Red Wings, the Detroit Drive and all the other things he owns. "Every hour that I put in here will be out of love. It won't feel like work. This whole thing is a labor of love."

Now. We can only hope that Ilitch doesn't get his parade rained on by the realities of 1992 baseball. Many a new owner has sniffed the stadium grass and stood on the pitcher's mound and proclaimed, "Wow, this is the greatest!"—and a few years later, he is holding his head and moaning, "Why did I ever get into this business?"

It could happen—even to Ilitch. The greed of the players, the egos of the owners, the expense of a stadium, the fickle nature of fans, all could conspire to wipe the smile off an owner's face. Admit this is true. But there was no removing that smile Wednesday afternoon. Not from that chiseled, curly-haired face that now owns one hundred percent of the major sports teams that play in this city.

"I'm not a savior of anything," Ilitch warned. "All the things I've done, if you broke them down, you'd see a lot of it was the people behind me. . . . But I'm excited. I want to bring baseball back to where it once was with this franchise. I'll probably spend every spare minute I have here. This is the game I love."

While he spoke, a waiter moved through the crowd holding a silver tray with slices of dessert. "Piece of cake?" the waiter asked. "Piece of cake?"

Not really. It only felt that way.

Charlie Gehringer ranked among the best second basemen in history—and among the most legendary of Tigers. Raised in Fowlerville, Michigan, he spent his entire career with Detroit, first as a player, then as a team executive. His uniform number, two, was retired by the team.

1993

Shirley Povich

QUIET GREATNESS

The other day when Charlie Gehringer died, it was so noted on television, briefly. And it did get some scattered recognition in the obituary sections. But for reasons most mystifying, it was ignored in the sports pages of many of the nation's newspapers, including *The Washington Post* and *New York Times.* Virtually no mention at all.

Altogether, it was a scanty and inadequate final salute to one of the genuine hero-figures of baseball, one of its most superb performers. Charlie Gehringer deserved more and better. At Cooperstown, even in the company of the Hall of Fame's most famous, his plaque glitters.

That the death of Charlie Gehringer, at eighty-nine, was given the brush-off probably speaks to the new values of the sports media. Television and the sports pages would have screamed the news if a Michael Jordan revealed that he had a slow-growth hangnail.

Among the most deprived of the nation's baseball fans were those born too late to see Charlie Gehringer play second

Charlie Gehringer

175

base and go to bat for the Detroit Tigers for nineteen years (1924–42). He could do it all, with style, while putting up the numbers that would make him a Hall of Fame shoo-in. Abner Doubleday, if indeed he invented the game, would have scripted Gehringer as the very model of the baseball athlete, with an eye-catching physique that belonged in a big league uniform—180 sculpted pounds, shoulders properly sloping, the legs tapered well, the cap worn just barely rakish. And owning all the skills to justify the image. Gehringer was the compleat player.

Back in October, in a thoughtless moment when *Sports Illustrated* offered its version of Baseball's Dream Team, I approved its selection of Jackie Robinson as the second baseman. It was an aberration. I want to retract it, and *Sports Illustrated* should too. Sacrilegious as it may seem, Jackie Robinson for all his abilities did not belong in the same league as Charlie Gehringer.

Could Gehringer hit? Better than Robinson; nine points better over a far longer career (.320). Did Robinson ever hit .371 and lead the league (his best was .342) as Gehringer did in 1937 (MVP in his fourteenth year in the majors)? Yes, Robinson was faster, but you couldn't say Gehringer (327 stolen bases) was slow.

All of this is not to denigrate Robinson—a great one—but unlike Gehringer he never hit twenty homers nor forty-nine doubles nor nineteen triples in a season, nor gave the impression of looking down the pitcher's throat as did Gehringer at bat. As a big-hitting second baseman, Rogers Hornsby and Eddie Collins and Nap Lajoie could be classed with Gehringer but nobody else.

Gehringer was a distinctive hitter, standing up there left-handed, and almost straight, and unlike any other batter he had the habit of following even the pitches he didn't offer at, turning his head to watch them settle into the catcher's mitt. Mystified catchers looked back at this curious guy.

It was Lefty Gomez who, in Gomez-style, paid Gehringer this tribute, "All I know is that when I'm pitching, he's always on base."

But it was Wes Ferrell, fifteen years in the majors, who perhaps said it best of Gehringer: "He was the toughest hitter I ever faced. He never offered to hit the first pitch. . . . You'd throw it in there and he'd just stand there and follow it into the catcher's mitt. . . . Sometimes he'd spot you two strikes and you couldn't get him out. He'd hit that ball and he'd beat you ball games. Yes he would."

That brings us to Charlie Gehringer's glove. How good was it? Good enough to put him up there in lights as the second baseman who led the AL in fielding eight times. If he made the plays look easy, silky-smooth, credit it to the way he positioned himself against batters like the student of the game he was.

In 1935, when Buddy Myer of the Senators beat Joe Vosmik out for the batting title by a fraction of a point with four hits on the last day, he said, "It would have been easy if Charlie Gehringer didn't take ten points off my average with all the hits he stole from me."

Charlie Gehringer didn't know how to strut. He was known as baseball's quiet man, content to let his bat and glove speak for him. With both he was an artist. His kind did not come along very often. His passing should have been better noted.

Sparky Anderson served as Detroit manager for most of seventeen seasons—longer than anyone in Tigers history. As Mike Lupica suggested in this column in 1995, Anderson's tenure in the Old English D was almost over.

1995
Mike Lupica

SPARKY

Maybe it is his last season, and the next time Sparky Anderson walks away from baseball he walks away for good. He will do this with his head high, a big guy to the end, after more than 2,000 wins, after winning the World Series in both leagues, after a career as a manager that puts him with

immortals, and always will have him talked about with the best. He is sixty-one years old, and Sparky Anderson says that it has taken this long into his baseball life not to be scared of the one thing that always scared him the most: a life outside baseball.

Because he has walked away from it now. Anderson walked away from replacement baseball last spring when other managers only talked about doing that. He went home to California and played golf and spent time with his grandchildren and traveled a little bit to Arizona. And Anderson says there was a day in March when he

Sparky Anderson

178

came home and told his wife he could quit the game for good if it came to that. There was still all this talk at the time that he would be fired when the strike ended, if it ever ended. And Anderson always wanted to make sure that he left on his own terms.

"I said to Carol, 'Should I just call them up on the phone and tell them I'm retiring?'" Anderson was saying yesterday afternoon, behind his desk in the visitors clubhouse at Yankee Stadium, filling the bowl of his pipe. "And she said, 'Now what brought this on?' And I said to her, 'I realized today I ain't afraid no more.'"

Anderson had the pipe the way he wanted it and now began to work on it with a match. His voice is still gravel and his hair still is white. When he finally is gone from baseball, it will seem that he always looked old, even when he was the young manager of the Big Red Machine. He is the closest thing baseball has had to Casey Stengel since Stengel himself, his genius never measured in syntax or good grammar. Now Anderson really is old in a young man's game. The manager at the other end of the hall, Buck Showalter of the Yankees, has not reached forty.

"I just wasn't afraid no more," he said yesterday. "Even in all the years when I had teams winning all those games, when they were calling me some kind of genius which is what they'll do when you got the horses, I was only afraid of one thing, and that was what I'd do when I couldn't manage my team anymore. What I'd do with myself. But then I walked away and found out that I could survive. I didn't want that to be the end of me in baseball. I didn't want that to be the way I went out. But I knew I could handle it now."

He leaned back in his chair and smoked his pipe. He had come into Yankee Stadium with a 28-28 baseball team, in a season when the Tigers weren't supposed to have a chance to do anything.

"Now I know that baseball can't tell me when I have to quit," he said. "There's a river everybody has to cross at some point in their life, and that river is the one with fear running through it. I crossed it when I refused to manage those replacement players. It was something I had to do, even if it made the hierarchy mad. I just never dreamed when I did it that I'd be ending the fear I'd always carried with me."

He has always talked this way. He has always made everything out to be a great drama. Sometimes he has anointed young ballplayers for Cooperstown right before those ballplayers ended up in Triple-A. But he came into Yankee Stadium last night with a .500 team that wasn't supposed to be anywhere close to that this season. He came in with 2,162 wins in the big leagues, third all-time. He has been the greatest baseball manager of his time.

When he walked away from replacement baseball, he seemed more a giant than he had ever been. He had managed nearly a quarter of a century and done too much and seen too much to join this kind of insult to his game. The people who run the Tigers didn't like it. There were other managers who thought it was nothing more than a grandstand play.

But in the end the Tigers did the smart thing, the only right thing, and took him back. Now all baseball finds out that the old man has lost nothing.

"I'm having the most fun I've had in seven years," he said yesterday. "And we're going to have more fun before this thing is over. There's going to be some bad times, too. But it's going to be a fun year."

The Tigers had won four in a row before last night and twelve of their last sixteen. Anderson has gotten hitting from everywhere, from Cecil Fielder and Alan Trammell, who have carried the Tigers for years, and from the likes of Juan Samuel and Chad Curtis and a catcher with some pop in his bat named John Flaherty. He still is looking for enough pitching to make a run in the American League East. It seems as if he has been looking for pitching since the last time the Tigers were in the playoffs in 1987. But Sparky Anderson still is here, twenty-four seasons after he was the kind of bright young manager, the kind of comer, Showalter is now with the Yankees.

"I was proud when I went home [this spring] when I did," Anderson said, "but I sure am glad that I'm back."

He stayed around long enough after the Big Red Machine to see a World Series canceled because of a strike. He stayed around long enough to see the owners try to sell replacement baseball to the fans of Florida and Arizona and threaten to bring it into the regular season. People wanted to know why he didn't make his stand earlier, but Anderson kept hoping that baseball wouldn't really put scabs on the field, that the game would never be shamed that way.

When the game was shamed, Sparky Anderson called a news conference in Lakeland one day and then went home. He left the ballpark and it felt as if one hundred people had left.

"Whatever happened," Anderson said, "I knew I was right and they were wrong."

He was asked who "they" were and Anderson smiled.

"All them guys who did what they did to baseball," he said.

Now baseball is back and so is Anderson, managing another flawed Tigers team and trying to give it a chance. As he spoke yesterday, it sounded as if the season was just beginning for him. He picked up the attendance figures from around baseball on Sunday and found enough big numbers to give him hope. He made you believe that somehow everything will be all right. He always has been able to do that with his players, all the way back.

"If I hadn't of come back," he said, "I wouldn't of gotten the chance to work with some of these kids." He smiled again, and said, "Which is the part that always keeps you young."

It was not much of a spring for Sparky Anderson. He believes the summer will be better. Even if it is the last summer.

Copyright 1995, Daily News. *Reprinted with permission.*

No two names in Tigers history are as entwined as those of Alan Trammell and Lou Whitaker, the heart of the Detroit infield for much of twenty years. Whitaker and Trammell rose to the major leagues together and departed within a year of each other. This piece appeared as Whitaker was playing his last season; Trammell stayed for the one after, as well.

1995

Jerry Green

TRAM AND WHITAKER

They were two strangers with fielders' gloves and identical dreams. They were joined, not by fate, but by a faltering baseball franchise in the autumn of 1976.

"We were in St. Petersburg, Fla., instructional baseball," said Lou Whitaker nineteen years later, on a special afternoon this past week. "That was the first time I ever met Tram."

 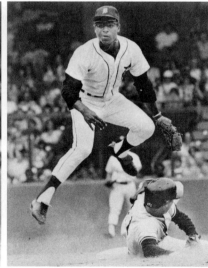

"A hotel room," recalled Alan Trammell, this same special afternoon. "I believe it was the Edgewater Hyatt. That was the day before instructional ball started."

"Tram was a hippy back then," said Whitaker, seated in the Tigers' clubhouse at the corner locker that traditionally belongs to the senior member of the ballclub. "Tram came out of high school with long hair. With hard rock music. Tram was a hippy. He loved that heavy metal. He's quieted down quite a bit from the first time that I met him."

"Oh, not," said Trammell, the co–senior member of the ballclub, at his locker down the row from Whitaker's. "They saw pictures of me in high school with long hair. When I went to Bristol, I can remember the first haircut I got there. I asked for a trim and the guy buzzed me. Rock 'n' roll? I grew up in California. It was the '70s. That's my California upbringing."

The Detroit Tigers were stuck in the middle of four successive failed seasons in 1976. The year before, when they signed Lou Whitaker and he started rising through the farm system, the club had lost 102 games and finished 37 ½ games out of first place. The following year, when they signed Alan Trammell, the big-league club improved to 87 losses and finished 24 games out of first place.

"I was making that switch," said Whitaker, who had played for the Lakeland farm club that season of '76. "I was a third baseman at the time, and they wanted to see if I could play second base."

"Right from the get-go, they moved him to second base," said Trammell, the shortstop. "I remember taking a lot of ground balls together and working extremely hard. Lou had it a little harder because he was being converted."

They came from opposite coasts. Whitaker, born in New York, learned his baseball on the fields of rural Virginia. Trammell, the southern Californian with the long-hair image, grew up in San Diego as a die-hard sports fan who collected autographs of visiting major leaguers and would slip under the fence of the Padres' ballpark to get into ballgames.

From different environments, of different races, with different personalities, Whitaker, then 19, and Trammell, then 18, were united by happenstance that autumn 19 years ago. They met in the hotel room. In that room other young farmhand ballplayers—Jack Morris, Lance Parrish, Dan Petry and Dave Rozema—also were receiving their orientation into the Florida Instructional League.

Trammell and Whitaker—Whitaker and Trammell—they would

remain united for nearly the next two decades. They would become the longest-standing second baseman–shortstop combination in the 120-year history of baseball. They would play more games as teammates than any other two players in the 95-year history of the American League.

Who put them together? "To be honest, I don't know," Trammell said. "Our farm director back then was Hoot Evers. Jim Campbell was the general manager. Bill Lajoie was in the organization as a scout. To be honest, I never found out."

The morning after Trammell and Whitaker met for the first time in the Edgewater Hyatt, they reported to Miller Huggins Field. They put on their uniforms. The brain trust of the Detroit ballclub was seated in the grandstands, talking baseball.

"We were sitting in the stands at third base," recalled Jim Campbell, the retired boss of the Tigers. "Kat (Ed Katalinas, head of the minor league organization), Rick Ferrell (the wise superscout), Hoot and myself. Trammell was beautiful. Whitaker was outstanding. We had no second baseman to play with Trammell.

"I said, 'Why don't we put Whitaker at second base?' But Kat blew up like a skyrocket. But he took to second base like a duck to water. It was a group decision: We tried it and it worked. It was just going to be a one-day experiment."

The one-day experiment on an instructional baseball infield has lasted nearly two decades, producing two decades of achievement. One year after they had been united by chance they would be in the big leagues together. They were worked hard that autumn of '76 by the manager of the Detroit team in the Instructional League.

"Les Moss was the manager," Trammell said. "Eddie Brinkman was an infielder instructor. . . . Then we ended up playing for Eddie the next year. He was the manager of Montgomery of the Southern League in '77."

In '77, the major-league Tigers lost 88 games and finished 26 games out. Tito Fuentes was the second baseman, Tom Veryzer the shortstop. Whitaker and Trammell were called up from Montgomery to the big leagues in September.

They made their major-league debuts in union, in the second game of a doubleheader at Fenway Park in Boston. Whitaker batted second and got a hit in his first at-bat in the majors, off Reggie Cleveland of the Red Sox. Trammell batted ninth and got a hit in his first major-league at-bat, off Cleveland. Whitaker finished his first game 3-for-5, with a double, one run batted in. Trammell went 2-for-3.

They had been joined in the majors. And in 1978, having skipped the

Triple A level of the minors, they would be the regular shortstop–second baseman combination for manager Ralph Houk's Tigers. Morris and Parrish would be fellow rookies on that club. Whitaker would be voted the American League's rookie of the year.

The Tigers' progress toward the 1984 championship had begun. The '78 club finished ten games over .500. And at the end of the season Houk resigned as manager.

Les Moss, who had first assembled Trammell and Whitaker on the field in the Instructional League, became their new manager in 1979. And on June 12 of that season, Jim Campbell fired Moss so he could hire Sparky Anderson, available and sought by several other clubs after his discharge by the Cincinnati Reds.

"The first time I saw them, when I was with Cincinnati at spring training in 1978, they were what I call balsa wood hitters," Anderson said this past week. "Lou hit balls between the third base bag and shortstop. He couldn't even get them over the shortstop. And Tram, he hit everything to right field. I said, 'My Lord, these two guys can really field, but they can't hit the ball very hard.'

"And exactly two years later, I'll never forget, they just grew up, both of them, and both of them could hit the ball out of the park. And Gates Brown said, I'll always remember what Gater said, he said, 'Those two boys have become men.' And from 1981 on, shoooo, they were just the dominating factor on this club from 1981 on. Defensively and offensively."

It could never be totally perfect.

Whitaker and Trammell were involved in two of Sparky Anderson's more historically eminent remarks. In the spring of 1985, Sparky sought to break up Trammell and Whitaker. A rookie named Chris Pittaro caught Anderson's imagination. Pittaro was a second baseman. Anderson, at spring training, announced that he was so enchanted with Pittaro that he was making him Trammell's new partner and that Whitaker was being switched to third base.

"Pittaro will play second base here for the next ten years," Sparky told us. "That's etched in stone."

Whitaker, quietly, typically not showing any emotion, accepted the transfer.

Next day, at the batting cage at Marchant Stadium in Lakeland, Whitaker softly, without anger, told this writer how upset he was about being switched to third base, that he was a second baseman, and that he wanted to continue to play second. When the column in *The Detroit News* reached Sparky, he reversed himself. Pittaro was shifted to third base, and soon would be gone from the Tigers. Whitaker was returned home to second base.

Whitaker and Trammell, joined together, were etched in stone.

But then at another spring training, Trammell's shoulder went bad. The velocity of his throws diminished. He was aching. And again he complained to this writer that he was being toyed about with mind games.

"Pain don't hurt you," said Sparky when asked about Trammell's injury in the rickety old ballpark at Fort Myers.

In 1987, the Tigers, with a spurt in the final week of the season, ignited by a home run by Kirk Gibson, caught up with the Blue Jays during the last weekend. The clubs tied for first place on Saturday, Trammell's sharply hit ball winning the game. The next day the Tigers, behind Frank Tanana, beat the Blue Jays 1-0 to win the division and qualify for the pennant playoffs.

That year Trammell batted .343 with 28 home runs, 205 hits, 105 RBI. Yet, when the voting for MVP was tabulated, he finished second to George Bell, who had vanished during the Blue Jays late-season collapse and was deeply responsible for them not winning the division.

It was an injustice—but Trammell still has his own trophy.

As Tanana flipped the come-backer from Garth Iorg underhand to Darrell Evans at first to clinch the division in the 1-0 game, Whitaker dashed for second base. He yanked the bag, with its stanchion, from the infield earth.

The other Tigers were jumping in celebration atop Tanana, the traditional clinching photo opportunity. In the clubhouse, Whitaker took the second base bag and presented it to his partner, Trammell.

"That was not common for Lou to do something like that," Trammell said this past week. "But it meant a lot. I'll remember that forever. While we were jumping in the pile he's grabbing the bag to give to me. That's the highlight I'll remember."

Trammell brought that base, now part of his living room adornments, to the ballpark the other day. On it, Lou Whitaker had written to Alan Trammell:

2B This year's MVP
Alan Trammell
Congratulations
Louis Rodman Whitaker

Sparky Anderson, with his eye toward baseball history and his feeling for nostalgia, will play Whitaker and Trammell together twice more. They'll play short and second, joined, Thursday in the season's finale at Tiger Stadium—and then in the last game at Baltimore.

They meshed so beautifully for so long, their double plays so graceful and precisioned, yet their personalities remain so different even now.

Whitaker was asked if he felt a sense of historical significance, playing so long alongside Trammell.

"I really don't think about it that much," he said. "I only think about playing. Of course, I'm not playing that much so I guess I can think about history. I just play the game. I'll always do that. When I'm finished playing baseball, then I'll think about those other things."

Same question to Trammell.

"We're in the record books for something and any time you do that, it's special," said Trammell. "It boils down to we've done the job for a long period of time. . . . We've been known always as a tandem. It's always been Lou and me, not one or the other. It's been both of us and I think that's something special."

The games will go on next season, most probably without Trammell and Whitaker.

Whitaker announced that 1995 was his final season last spring, and in September is not certain. "I don't know what I'm going to do," Whitaker said. "I'll wait and see what happens over the winter. If I'm in shape I might play. If I'm not in shape I won't play. It'll take me too long to get back in shape. The only thing I can be now is a pinch hitter, play a little second base."

Trammell, down the row of lockers in the clubhouse, tugged at his shirt and said he would make no announcement until after the season. "I'm afraid to take this uniform off," he said. "I knew it would be hard for me since I'm such a sports guy, and the game meant so much to me that I think it'll be easier when the season's over and I have a little more time to reflect and not go to the ballpark on a daily basis and put the uniform on.

"I don't have the heart to do it while I have the uniform on. It'll be easier then for me to say it's over. In all honesty, it is."

When you edit a collection such as this, your publisher expects you to include one of your own pieces. So, I humbly offer this excerpt from The Final Season, *my memoir of the last year at Tiger Stadium.*

1999
Tom Stanton

THE FINAL SEASON

Eighty-seven years earlier on a Saturday in April 1912, days after the *Titanic* sank, the Detroit ball club played its first game on this diamond. It was called Navin Field and it was about half the size then, jammed with more than 24,300 fans. Cleveland's "Shoeless Joe" Jackson scored the inaugural run and Ty Cobb responded a half-inning later by stealing home. The Tigers won 6-5 in eleven innings, christening a field that over the decades has hosted all the greats: Ruth and Gehrig, DiMaggio and Williams, Mantle, Mays and Aaron, Nolan Ryan and Roger Clemens. Boston's Fenway Park opened the same day. They are America's oldest ballparks.

It was that year on a Tuesday in July when Theodore Stankiewicz, a twenty-six-year-old welder, married Anna Tuchewicz at St. Hyacinth Church in Detroit, beginning a union that would produce ten children and a thousand stories. Teddy, as pals called him, had fled Poland after being drafted into the German army. He followed his two brothers, who at six foot five stood nearly a foot

Tiger Stadium

taller. We know little about his life in Europe, except that he grew up on a farm and lost his father early. Anna, Teddy's bride, was eighteen. She worked in a cigar factory and like her younger siblings lived with her parents, a stern Catholic couple from Europe. Nine months after the wedding, they began their family. First Clem was born, then Edward, Theodore, and Irene. While expecting her fifth baby in early 1920, Anna took ill and lost her eyesight. She spent months in bed, watched over by her sisters and mother, saying rosaries and praying to Saint Anne to save her child, telling God that while she might not be worthy of His mercy, the baby should be spared. For Anna, every joy and every tragedy found its roots in her faith. In March when the child was born, her sight returned. She pronounced both miracles and bestowed upon her son, my father, the most sacred name she could imagine, Joseph Marion.

Generations of Detroiters have watched baseball at Michigan and Trumbull avenues. My grandfather cheered Cobb and "Wahoo" Sam Crawford. As a teen in the 1930s, my dad packed peanuts beneath the bleachers for a chance to behold the G-Men: Gehringer, Greenberg, and Goslin. Later he took me to see Kaline. Now I take my sons and they have their own favorites. The tradition is not unique to us.

Game time is a good hour away when Bobby Higginson strides to the bench after batting practice, his unsmiling lips framed by a tight goatee.

"Hand this to him," he says, pointing the barrel of his black baseball bat at an unsuspecting boy two rows back. Higginson, an intense right fielder prone to outbursts, slides the cracked bat over the glossy roof of the Tiger dugout. He pauses, watching that it gets to Mickey Bozymowski, and disappears down the steps into the clubhouse.

The boy holds the bat like a sacred sword. He caresses its neck, sticky with pine tar, and looks up to his dad, who says, "Oh, man!" Michael Bozymowski has been a baseball fan since the 1960s. "Oh, man!" he says. "I don't believe this."

The team's most popular player has anointed Michael Bozymowski's son, at the home opener no less. Does Higginson realize that he has etched a moment into one family's history—that in sixty years Mickey Bozymowski will be recalling this day for his grandchildren? Mickey's dad knows it. He grins, shakes his head, and lets his eyes drift over the grass field.

"I just had to be here," he says.

Nearby, Alan Trammell, the former shortstop and first-year batting coach, gives autographs at the edge of the dugout and a knot of fans tightens toward him. In 1978 as I was finishing high school, Trammell was beginning his first full season. He and Lou Whitaker were the Gold-dust Twins. On this Monday in spring, with his shades perched on the bill of his ball cap, he looks younger than forty-one. He is trim and boyish in the face. The acne scars of his youth have smoothed.

"You the man, Al," someone shouts.

Trammell signs a baseball and politely excuses himself. "I've got to go to work now," he says, as if he needs to explain.

The park is a circus of sound. The click of ball meeting bat echoes from the batting cage. The Jumbotron screen over center field blares highlights of last year's Sammy Sosa–Mark McGwire home run race.

"Ice cold beer," yells an unpracticed vendor, the words strange on his tongue. "Wash down the pretzels. Wash down that popcorn. Ice cold beer."

Few are buying yet. The veteran, Art Witkosky, knows this. He resembles a white-haired Johnny Cash and the only thing he is selling at this moment is himself. Witkosky hoists a bag of buns above his head, posing for the press. Though he's been hawking hot dogs since Nixon's presidency, Witkosky never tires of opening day.

Above home plate in the WJR radio booth, Hall of Famer Ernie Harwell prepares for his broadcast. Harwell is one of my boyhood idols, a fatherly figure I listened to in bed in the dark on late summer evenings, with the Tigers playing on the West Coast and the signal coming in clear on the transistor radio and the crickets chirping outside my window. I imagine him a considerate man and I hope to meet him. Callously fired years earlier, Harwell, eighty-one, has returned to do play-by-play, his fortieth Detroit season. In a Greek sailor's cap and tan overcoat, he settles into the open-air booth behind fencing that protects him from foul balls, lest he meet the fate of H. G. Salsinger, the late sportswriter who took a blinding ball to the face in 1954 and never returned to the park.

Today Harwell's unhurried voice, hinting at his Georgia childhood, floats from the radio, slow and sweet and sincere as a mother's praise.

"Baseball greetings, everybody, from The Corner. It'll be the last time we say that on an opening day. This is a great occasion, and the weatherman has blessed us with some good weather. It is sunny. It's not warm; it's cool. But it's sunny and we are very thankful for that."

Wind snaps the American League team pennants that line the roof of the stadium like flags atop a castle. Tiger Stadium is a double-deck fortress, the only major-league park encircled by two levels of stands. From almost all seats you can see nothing outside the park, no landmarks, no buildings, no cars. Just the sky, the seagulls, and several planes circling above trailing banners that read, *Think Ford First, Ron's Body Shop and Suspension* and *Deja Vu's Totally Nude Showgirls.*

In the upper deck along the right-field foul line, it is cold in the shade, colder than the announced game-time temperature of forty-seven degrees. Fans with ski hats and winter gloves struggle to get warm. A woman trudges up the narrow chipped steps in a fuzzy feline costume, and my dad gives her a second look.

He sits to my right so I can talk into his hearing aid. He's got eyeglasses as big as flight goggles. Somehow you can see the kid in him.

"Never been up here before," he says.

Dad has been coming to games since the 1920s when his father bought tickets with the extra change he earned brewing coffee during lunch breaks at the Chrysler plant. In Poland Theodore Stankiewicz had never heard of baseball. In America he worshiped it, spending more time at ball fields than in the eastside Catholic churches where his children were baptized. When he arrived in America, the Tigers played at Bennett Park, named for Charlie Bennett, a star catcher who lost his legs in a streetcar accident. Bennett Park came down in 1911, replaced by the larger Navin Field, to accommodate the burgeoning city of immigrants and the demand to see Ty Cobb, the American League's top hitter and fiercest competitor. The park expanded several times, doubling in size by 1938 and taking the last name of new owner Walter Briggs.

It was Briggs Stadium when Harold "Prince Hal" Newhouser made it to the big leagues in 1939 after his senior year in high school. Newhouser lived in the city and starred on local teams. Before he became a pro he had pitched for Roose-Vanker, the American Legion state champions. My dad batted against him in a single game that has become part of family legend.

Two years ago Dad, my brother, and I came for the retirement of Newhouser's uniform number, sixteen. On the drive down Dad said he felt like a boy. Then he paused, stared off through the tinted car window and exhaled with a subtle, satisfying "hmmm."

"Sometimes when I'm shaving, I don't recognize myself in the mirror," he said. "I see an old man."

For the ceremony Dad stood by the dugout, camera in hand. When Newhouser, in poor health, stepped onto the field, Dad edged closer to the diamond. I think he hoped that his former adversary would spot him in the crowd of thousands and recognize him as the wily second baseman who sixty years earlier had spoiled his sandlot no-hitter with two bloop hits that rolled into the crowd for ground-rule doubles. Weeks earlier, before the ceremony, Dad had sent him a letter recalling their encounter. Who could expect Newhouser to remember? He had gone on to face some of baseball's best hitters. He had gone on to pitch in All-Star games and the World Series. He had even been the American League's Most Valuable Player—twice.

But before all that, when he was a fast-throwing phenom, he had had to face my dad and my dad had gotten the better of him. Grandpa Stankiewicz watched that scrub game with a cigar in his hand and two in his shirt pocket. He took pride in his son's hits.

"You swung on a line, Joe," he said.

Newhouser died last November. (He never did answer Dad's letter.) But his number hangs on the facing of the third deck and whenever I look at it I think of my father.

In the bleachers awash in sunshine, shirtless young men punch beach balls into the breeze. Occasionally one drifts onto the field, halting the scoreless game between Willie Blair and Minnesota's Eric Milton. Some shutouts arise from precise control, an over-powering fastball, or a nice mix of pitches; others result from lousy hitting. That's the case today and there is no worse scenario for an opener. The stands are packed with party-goers who hunger for celebration, not baseball. They'd be as happy at a demolition derby if there was beer. And I resent them for it because this should be a solemn, respectful time, not an excuse to get drunk.

A well-endowed woman flutters the bottom of her blouse, baiting the men who sit nearby. The fans to her right cheer. She looks to her left and swirls her arms into the air. The hoots and applause grow again. Inspired, she frolics into the aisle and fulfills her promise, festively hoisting her top over her jiggling head. Her admirers boo as police escort her from the park. One tosses a roll of toilet paper over the guardrail. It unfurls, a white, three-ply ribbon.

In the late innings several college-age men leap the outfield fences and dart onto the field, easily evading the middle-aged security guards who take care not to flop before a sellout crowd of over forty-seven thousand. One intruder trips near the Budweiser sign in left-center. Another slides bare-chested and headfirst into second base.

Everyone wants to be a star.

If this were a movie, Bobby Higginson would be at the plate with another black bat and Mickey Bozymowski would be big-eyed and hopeful. Instead, it's Damion Easley, the second baseman, who finds himself where every ball-playing kid dreams of glory: bottom of the ninth, two out, the winning run on third and the count at three balls, two strikes. Easley is poised to be the hero. The fans can feel it. They rise from their seats, their cheers building to thunder. But the not-so-mighty Easley strikes out.

Relief pitcher Todd Jones, with his bleached-blond goatee, enters in the tenth inning. He has Al Kaline's Wilson A-2000 glove, the same glove Kaline used in 1974, his final season. "I just think something of his needs to be on that field," Jones said earlier. He pitches flawlessly. His successor, though, surrenders a twelfth-inning home run and the Tigers lose, their sixth straight defeat following a dismal start on the road.

"Tough loss," says Dad, as if I were a kid again who needed consoling. On some level, I do. But not about the game.

Excerpted from The Final Season *by Tom Stanton, copyright 2001,*
published by Thomas Dunne Books/St. Martin's Press.
Reprinted with permission.

As the Tigers of 2003 tumbled toward infamy, the national media began to take notice. Despite the dire predictions in this Time Magazine *piece, Detroit averted disaster by winning several of its last games, sparing the club the designation of worst team of the modern era. That distinction still belongs to the 1962 New York Mets.*

2003

Joel Stein

BEAUTIFUL LOSERS?

The problem isn't that the Detroit Tigers are about to become the losingest team in modern major league history. The problem is that they're doing it wrong. The 1962 Mets, whose 40-120 record is likely to be eclipsed by Detroit this week, were lovable losers. They were a brand-new expansion team with, in those pre–Toronto Raptors days, the dumbest team name ever conceived. Not only did the Mets have a mascot that was just a baseball with a face drawn on it, but they named the mascot Mr. Met. Everyone knew the Mets were going to stink, and they stank with wild abandon. Despite the losses they ranked sixth in attendance that year. They were all ridiculous fun, the UPN of their time, and they pitched like they were pitching the premise for *Homeboys in Outer Space.*

But the Tigers are in complete denial. They are trudging through their ineptitude without a sly wink, convinced they are getting Jobed every night. But unless they pull off a miracle in the next week, they will have the most losses in modern major league history. They were statistically eliminated from winning their

division on Aug. 22. And that's the American League Central, a division most people don't know even exists. Their owner has decided the team is so unimportant that he's spending more money on the payroll of his hockey team, which plays a sport most people don't know exists.

The Tigers' sole nod to their lameness was hiring Mike Veeck, the son of Bill Veeck, the Hall of Fame owner who organized the disco-album bonfire at Comiskey Park in the '70s, to do their promotions. So they did have Duct Tape Night, Magic Night with illusionist Aaron Radatz, a Christian concert after an Angels game and Baseball Card Blitz, where kids under 15 got to trample one another on a field littered with 50,000 packs of baseball cards. But Veeck didn't go far enough. First of all, he should have removed the Tigers from those baseball-card packs. And he should have replaced the entire lineup with Tiger look-alike midgets, signed Rickey Henderson, put patches of the still living Al Kaline on their sleeves and accidentally blown a water main in their lame new ballpark so the team could have finished the season in its original home, Tiger Stadium.

But the real problem is that Veeck's attitude didn't trickle down to the young, boring, serious team with its radio-face manager, Alan Trammell. Unlike the 1962 Mets, who had "Choo Choo" Coleman and "Don" Zimmer, the Tigers don't have one player with a decent nickname. Trammell refuses to talk about the Mets' record 120 losses, telling a *Time* reporter much gutsier than I am, "I'm not going to answer that question." Not that the reporter was brave for asking Trammell but for sitting through the entire game.

What no one on the team understands is that being oblivious to how you are perceived is the easiest path to unlikability. The lovable loser knows he's hopelessly failing, while the plain old loser keeps up the ugly charade. And although ignoring reality may seem dignified, it's really like Michael Dukakis' riding in the tank and thinking it made him look like a warrior. The lovable loser has more dignity because he keeps going despite his awareness of futility: he knows it's stupid to raise taxes and not lose every state except Minnesota, to try to kick the football while Lucy's holding it, to think dropping the AOL part from his name will fool anybody—but he tries anyway.

What the Tigers also don't understand is that no one is disgusted by losing. If they did understand that, they wouldn't try to pretend it wasn't happening. There are 30 teams in baseball and each year the 29 of them that are not the Yankees lose. The Boston Red Sox, who haven't won a

World Series since 1918, aren't losers, because they play for the love of the game. I'm just kidding; the Red Sox are total losers. But even the Yankees aren't World Series champions in almost 75% of their seasons. Life is mostly losing. It's a series of imperfect essays full of jokes that don't quite work, of dreams that go unfulfilled, of passions that dwindle and ultimately, death. And if you don't figure out how to strive with the acceptance of guaranteed failure, how to find fulfillment in the eternal recurrence of imperfection, then you can have a brand-new stadium with a Ferris wheel, and no one is going to come. I'm rooting for the Tigers to win because they don't deserve to lose.

When Ivan "Pudge" Rodriguez signed with the Tigers prior to the start of the 2004 season, old-time baseball fans compared the move to the team's 1934 acquisition of star catcher Mickey Cochrane, who within two years would lead the Detroiters to a world title. Rodriguez didn't bring the team a pennant in his first year at Comerica Park, but he did lead the Tigers back toward respectability.

2004

Drew Sharp

PUDGE ARRIVES

LAKELAND, FL—Eager sixty-year-olds acted like restless six-year-olds in the backseat of the family car on an endless vacation drive.

"Is he here yet? Is he here yet?"

As noon Wednesday arrived, Ivan (Pudge) Rodriguez had yet to "officially" arrive at his new spring training home. Manager Alan Trammell had heard that the Tigers' big free-agent acquisition briefly stopped by Marchant Stadium on Tuesday night to check out the facilities after everyone was long gone.

"It won't be official until I see him walk through these gates," said one woman Wednesday who had been camped out at the clubhouse entrance since 8 A.M., "because I still won't really believe that he's actually here until I see him."

They saw him around 1 P.M. when his black Bentley pulled into the Marchant Stadium parking lot. Rodriguez saw the crowd of about sixty peo-

ple huddled around the main clubhouse entrance, so he swung around to the back. And about two-thirds of that throng followed in hot pursuit, surrounding the car so Rodriguez couldn't get out of the door.

The Tigers didn't get a catcher. They got a rock star. All that was missing was the shredding of clothing and the fainting spells.

The wild spontaneity of Pudge's first day further reminds us of how far this franchise has fallen into the wretched abyss and how badly the passionate want something—anything—to get excited about.

"I've never seen anything like that," said lifelong Lakeland resident Carlos Nava, who said he had been to every spring training opening in the past twenty years. "And these weren't all little kids chasing that car, either. It didn't make sense to me, but I guess people have been waiting a long time to feel good about the Tigers. And Pudge is a great player."

Even more important, Rodriguez seems comfortable with the trappings of instant demigod. He craves the superstar attention. If you wanted to slip in unannounced, you leave the Bentley in the garage and choose a mode of transportation that provides a tad more anonymity. He happily embraces his new responsibilities as the face and fury of this organization's anticipated renaissance.

It didn't take him long to realize how important his signing has been to Detroit. He was surprised when he received a standing ovation at the Palace during a Pistons game the day following his introductory news conference. He joked that it was a nice, warm welcome because it was much colder outside than he was accustomed to.

Pudge gets it.

He may be a Tiger today only because nobody else came close to matching the four years, $40 million that Mike Ilitch coughed up, but he has already adopted his team's horrendous effort the past three years as his own. It was interesting how he frequently used the word "we" when discussing the problems, not "they."

"We're in this together," he said. "If we stay together and remember that we're a family, we'll be a better team than last year."

Pudge proved more congenial in one hour than Juan Gonzalez did in one season. Gonzalez was constantly flanked by an array of stooges insulating him from prying eyes wishing to get a little closer to the team's newest star. But Pudge's "posse" consisted of one—his older brother, Jose. As he sat by his cubicle trying on his new uniform and equipment for fit, he invited the cameras to capture every minute detail. As he approached the batting cage to take a few practice strokes, he politely stopped and smiled so that a little boy with a camera could take a quick picture.

Most of his new teammates were gone for the day when he arrived. He's saving the introductions for today. But a few couldn't wait.

"Awright, you're here!" shouted another new Tiger, Rondell White, after he spotted Pudge. "Man, I'm so glad that you're on board, Dog!"

Trammell is still convincing himself that the future Hall of Famer is actually a Tiger.

"Honestly, I still can't believe it," he said. "The longer it took, the more I felt that he didn't want to come here. But it's been done for two weeks and I'm still asking myself if it actually happened. It isn't a dream. He's really here."

He's here and he's ready to get to work. He's not waiting for Trammell to tell him to speak up in the clubhouse. He's going to do it anyway because he knows leadership is but one of the many job descriptions the Tigers paid for when they signed that fat check.

"For us, this is big," Trammell said.

Qualifiers are necessary because the New York Yankees' trade for Alex Rodriguez this week has significantly broadened the definition of "big." A-Rod likely means another World Series championship for the Yankees, but I-Rod means the baseball world takes the Tigers a little more seriously.

And that's more than enough right now to generate some genuine excitement.

About the Editor

Tom Stanton has been a journalist for nearly three decades—and a Detroit Tigers fan for ten more.

He is the author of the Tiger Stadium memoir *The Final Season,* the only book to have won both the Casey and Elysian Fields Quarterly awards, given to the best baseball book of the year. He also wrote *The Road to Cooperstown: A Father, Two Sons and the Journey of a Lifetime,* as well as *Hank Aaron and the Home Run That Changed America.*

A founder and former owner of The Voice newspapers in suburban Detroit, he holds a master's degree from Michigan State University, received a prestigious Michigan Jouralism Fellowship, and served as a journalism professor at the University of Detroit Mercy. He resides in New Baltimore, Michigan, with his family. He can be reached through his website, www.tomstanton.com, or through the mail at PO Box 636, New Baltimore, MI 48047.

Grateful acknowledgment is given to the Burton Historical Collection, Detroit Public Library for permission to reproduce the following illustrations accompanying the articles (in order of appearance):

Ty Cobb, in "Dear Boy"
Frank Navin with Billy Sullivan, in "Life Is Short"
Navin Field, in "A New Home"
Ty Cobb and his children, in "A Day with Cobb"
Oscar Stanage, in "A Baseball Romance"
Sam Crawford, in "Germany the Jokester"
Schoolboy Rowe, in "Schoolboy"
Chief Hogsett, in "Yearning for Detroit"
Elden Auker, in "Game Four"
Goose Goslin, in "Victory Finally"
Buck Newsom, in "One for Dad"
Briggs Stadium, in "Satchel in the Park"
Harold "Prince Hal" Newhouser, in " 'Prince' Hal?"
Rocky Colavito, in "Harvey for Rocky"
Mickey Lolich and Billy Martin, in "The Pride Within"
Ralph Houk, in "One Bad Day"
Al Kaline and owner John Fetzer, in "On Kaline's Knee"
Willie Horton, in "Sentimental Willie"
Charlie Gehringer, in "Quiet Greatness"

Grateful acknowledgment is given to the National Baseball Hall of Fame and Museum, Inc., for permission to reproduce the illustrations for "Jack's Gem" and "Tram and Whitaker."

Grateful acknowledgment is also given to the following for permission to reproduce illustrations:

Christa Howard for the photograph of Sparky Anderson in "Sparky"
Scott Menig at www.MotownSports.com for the photograph of the coaches in "Beautiful Losers?"
Joy R. Absalon for the photograph in "Pudge Arrives"

The following photographs are by Tom Stanton:

Mark Fidrych, in "The Rookie"
Al Kaline, in "Thank You"
Ernie Harwell, in "A Lucky Man"
Alan Trammell, in "Worst Ever?"
1984 World Series Banner at Tiger Stadium, in "The Owner"
Left field roof at Tiger Stadium, in "Baby Babe"
Outside Tiger Stadium, in "The Final Season"

All other illustrations are from the author's personal collection.

Text design by Jillian Downey
Typesetting by Delmastype, Ann Arbor, Michigan
Text font: New Baskerville
Display fonts: Diamond and Eclat

"British printer John Baskerville of Birmingham created the types
that bear his name in about 1752. George Jones designed this version of Baskerville for Linotype-Hell in 1930, and the International
Typeface Corporation licensed it in 1982."
                                        —Courtesy www.adobe.com

Diamond is a FontBank font.

Eclat was designed by Doyald Young for Image Club Graphics in 1984.
                                        —Courtesy www.identifont.com